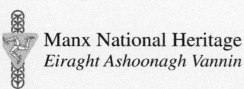

Manx National Heritage
Eiraght Ashoonagh Vannin

T0386651

RECOLLECTIONS OF THE
ISLE OF MAN INTERNATIONAL
SCOOTER RALLY

SCOOTER MANIA!

STEVE JACKSON
FOREWORDS BY MAU SPENCER & NORRIE KERR

Enthusiast's Restoration Manual Series
Beginner's Guide to Classic Motorcycle Restoration, The (Burns)
Classic Large Frame Vespa Scooters, How to Restore (Paxton)
Classic Small Frame Vespa Scooters, How to Restore (Paxton)
Classic Off-road Motorcycles, How to Restore (Burns)
Ducati Bevel Twins 1971 to 1986 (Falloon)
Honda CX500 & CX650, How to restore – YOUR step-by-step colour illustrated guide to complete restoration (Burns)
Honda Fours, How to restore – YOUR step-by-step colour illustrated guide to complete restoration (Burns)
Kawasaki Z1, Z/KZ900 & Z/KZ1000, How to restore (Rooke)
Norton Commando, How to Restore (Rooke)
Triumph Trident T150/T160 & BSA Rocket III, How to Restore (Rooke)
Yamaha FS1-E, How to Restore (Watts)

Biographies
Chris Carter at Large – Stories from a lifetime in motorcycle racing (Carter & Skelton)
Edward Turner – The Man Behind the Motorcycles (Clew)
Jim Redman – 6 Times World Motorcycle Champion: The Autobiography (Redman)
Mason's Motoring Mayhem – Tony Mason's hectic life in motorsport and television (Mason)
'Sox' – Gary Hocking – the forgotten World Motorcycle Champion (Hughes)

General
An Incredible Journey (Falls & Reisch)
Automotive A-Z, Lane's Dictionary of Automotive Terms (Lane)
Bluebird CN7 (Stevens)
BMW Boxer Twins 1970-1995 Bible, The (Falloon)
BMW Cafe Racers (Cloesen)
BMW Classic 5 Series 1972 to 2003 (Cranswick)
BMW Custom Motorcycles – Choppers, Cruisers, Bobbers, Trikes & Quads (Cloesen)
Bonjour – Is this Italy? (Turner)
British 250cc Racing Motorcycles (Pereira)
British Café Racers (Cloesen)
British Custom Motorcycles – The Brit Chop – choppers, cruisers, bobbers & trikes (Cloesen)
BSA Bantam Bible, The (Henshaw)
BSA Motorcycles – the final evolution (Jones)
Ducati 750 Bible, The (Falloon)
Ducati 750 SS 'round-case' 1974, The Book of the (Falloon)
Ducati 860, 900 and Mille Bible, The (Falloon)
Ducati Monster Bible (New Updated & Revised Edition), The (Falloon)
Ducati Story, The – 6th Edition (Falloon)
Ducati 916 (updated edition) (Falloon)
Fine Art of the Motorcycle Engine, The (Peirce)
Forza Minardi! (Vigar)
Franklin's Indians (Sucher/Pickering/Diamond/Havelin)
From Crystal Palace to Red Square – A Hapless Biker's Road to Russia (Turner)
Funky Mopeds (Skelton)
Honda NR500/NS500 'One Day We Will Win' – The Trials of Regaining the Motorcycle World Championship (Togashi)

India – The Shimmering Dream (Reisch/Falls (translator))
Italian Cafe Racers (Cloesen)
Italian Custom Motorcycles (Cloesen)
Kawasaki Triples Bible, The (Walker)
Kawasaki W, H1 & Z – The Big Air-cooled Machines (Long)
Kawasaki Z1 Story, The (Sheehan)
Lambretta Bible, The (Davies)
Laverda Twins & Triples Bible 1968-1986 (Falloon)
Lea-Francis Story, The (Price)
Little book of trikes, the (Quellin)
Mike the Bike – Again (Macauley)
Moto Guzzi Sport & Le Mans Bible, The (Falloon)
Moto Guzzi Story, The – 3rd Edition (Falloon)
Motorcycle Apprentice (Cakebread)
Motorcycle GP Racing in the 1960s (Pereira)
Motorcycle Racing with the Continental Circus 1920-1970 (Pereira)
Motorcycle Road & Racing Chassis Designs (Noakes)
Motorcycles and Motorcycling in the USSR from 1939 (Turbett)
Motorcycling in the '50s (Clew)
MV Agusta Fours, The book of the classic (Falloon)
The MV Agusta Story (Falloon)
Norton Commando Bible – All models 1968 to 1978 (Henshaw)
Off-Road Giants! (Volume 1) – Heroes of 1960s Motorcycle Sport (Westlake)
Off-Road Giants! (Volume 2) – Heroes of 1960s Motorcycle Sport (Westlake)
Off-Road Giants! (Volume 3) – Heroes of 1960s Motorcycle Sport (Westlake)
Peking to Paris 2007 (Young)
Preston Tucker & Others (Linde)
Racing Classic Motorcycles (Reynolds)
Racing Line – British motorcycle racing in the golden age of the big single (Guntrip)
The Red Baron's Ultimate Ducati Desmo Manual (Cabrera Choclán)
Scooters & Microcars, The A-Z of Popular (Dan)
Scooter Lifestyle (Grainger)
Scooter Mania! – Recollections of the Isle of Man International Scooter Rally (Jackson)
Singer Story: Cars, Commercial Vehicles, Bicycles & Motorcycle (Atkinson)
Slow Burn: the growth of Superbikes and Superbike racing 1970-1988 (Guntrip)
Suzuki Motorcycles - The Classic Two-stroke Era (Long)
This Day in Automotive History (Corey)
Triumph Bonneville Bible (59-83) (Henshaw)
Triumph Bonneville!, Save the – The inside story of the Meriden Workers' Co-op (Rosamond)
Triumph Motorcycles & the Meriden Factory (Hancox)
Triumph Speed Twin & Thunderbird Bible (Woolridge)
Triumph Tiger Cub Bible (Estall)
Triumph Trophy Bible (Woolridge)
Triumph TR6 (Kimberley)
TT Talking – The TT's most exciting era – As seen by Manx Radio TT's lead commentator 2004-2012 (Lambert)
Velocette Motorcycles – MSS to Thruxton – Third Edition (Burris)
Vespa – The Story of a Cult Classic in Pictures (Uhlig)
Vincent Motorcycles: The Untold Story since 1946 (Guyony & Parker)

www.veloce.co.uk

Cover photo: Left to right: D Wenham, P J Yates, and JN Jones are the riders in the driving seat competing at Douglas sand races. (MNH)

First published in May 2014, reprinted March 2021 by Veloce Publishing Limited, Veloce House, Parkway Farm Business Park, Middle Farm Way, Poundbury, Dorchester, Dorset, DT1 3AR, England.
Fax 01305 250479/e-mail info@veloce.co.uk/web www.veloce.co.uk or www.velocebooks.com.
ISBN: 978-1-845846-48-0 UPC: 6-36847-04648-4
© Steve Jackson and Veloce Publishing 2014 & 2021. All rights reserved. With the exception of quoting brief passages for the purpose of review, no part of this publication may be recorded, reproduced or transmitted by any means, including photocopying, without the written permission of Veloce Publishing Ltd. Throughout this book logos, model names and designations, etc, have been used for the purposes of identification, illustration and decoration. Such names are the property of the trademark holder as this is not an official publication.
Readers with ideas for automotive books, or books on other transport or related hobby subjects, are invited to write to the editorial director of Veloce Publishing at the above address.
British Library Cataloguing in Publication Data – A catalogue record for this book is available from the British Library.
Typesetting, design and page make-up all by Veloce Publishing Ltd on Apple Mac. Printed and bound by CPI Group (UK) Ltd, Croydon, CR0 4YY.

CONTENTS

Notes

1   *IOM Examiner,* 26 April 1957, p4
2   *IOM Examiner,* 12 April 1957, p1
3   21 May 1957, p3
4   *IOM Examiner,* 24 May 1957, p8
5   25 May 1957, p2
6   *The Motor Cycle,* 13 June 1957, p742 in bound copy Tourist Trophy reports MNH ref C498/2/11
7   11 June 1957, p5
8   *IOM Weekly Times,* 4 July 1957, p1
9   28 June 1957, p9
10 *IOM Weekly Times,* 23 August 1957, p1
11 *IOM Examiner,* 23 August 1957, p8
12 *Green Final,* 14 September 1957, p4
13 *Ramsey Courier,* 20 December 1957, p2
14 *Green Final,* 1 February 1958, p1
15 *IOM Weekly Times,* 16 May 1958, p1
16 29 April 1958, p1
17 *IOM Weekly Times,* 17 June 1958, p2
18 *IOM Weekly Times,* 13 June 1958, p1
19 *Motor Cycling,* 19 June 1958, p252
20 IOM Daily Times, 1 July 1958, p3
21 IOM Daily Times, 8 July 1958, p4
22 *IOM Weekly Times,* 31 October 1958, p1
23 *IOM Weekly Times,* 7 November 1958, p6
24 *IOM Daily Times,* 22 April 1959, p1
25 *IOM Examiner,* 4 Jun 1959
26 *IOM Examiner,* 11 June 1959, p1
27 *IOM Daily Times,* 16 June 1959, p6
28 *Green Final,* 22 August 1959, p4
29 IOM Daily Times, 30 September 1959, p7
30 *IOM Weekly Times,* 20 November 1959, p5
31 *Green Final,* 9 January 1960, p1
32 *Scooter and Three Wheeler,* August 1960, p66
33 *Scooter and Three Wheeler,* August 1960, p67
34 *IOM Daily Times,* 28 June 1960, p1& 3.
35 *Scooter and Three Wheeler,* August 1960, p69-70
36 1960 Isle of Man International Scooter Rally Regulations, p12
37 *Holiday News,* 1 July 1961, p4
38 *Motor Cycling with Scooter Weekly,* 6 July 1961, p320
39 *Mona's Herald,* February 13, p2
40 *Scooter and Three Wheeler,* August 1962
41 13 June 1962, p5
42 *Scooter and Three Wheeler,* August 1962, p36
43 *Daily Mail,* 13 June 1962, p5
44 *IOM Weekly Times,* June 15 1962, p1
45 14 June 1962, p7
46 *IOM Examiner,* 14 June 1962, p1
47 *Scooter and Three Wheeler,* September 1963, p35
48 24 June 1963, p10
49 *IOM Daily Times* and *Women's Magazine,* June 25 1963, p1
50 11 January 1964, p4
51 *IOM Weekly Times,* 26 June 1964, p11
52 September, 1964, 30
53 *IOM Daily Times,* June 28 1965, p1
54 *Scooter and Three Wheeler,* September 1965, p28-29
55 *Scooter and Three Wheeler,* September 1965, p28-29
56 *IOM Examiner,* 1 June 1967, p6
57 August 1967, p9
58 *Scooter and Three Wheeler,* August 1967, p10
59 *Scooter and Three Wheeler,* August 1967, p13
60 *Mona's Herald,* 4 July 1967, p4
61 *Holiday News,* no. 4, 22 June 1968, p1
62 *Scootering and Lightweights,* August 1968, p18
63 *Mona's Herald,* 2 July, 1968, p4
64 *Scootering and Lightweights,* August 1968, p14
65 *Scooter World,* August 1968, p11
66 *Scooter World,* August 1969, p15
67 *Scooter World,* August 1969, p16
68 *Scooter World,* August 1969, p18
69 *Scooter World,* August 1969, p25
70 *Daily Express,* 24 June 1970, p15
71 *Scooter World,* August 1970, p21
72 *Scooter World,* August 1970, p19
73 *Daily Express,* 23 June 1970
74 *IOM Courier,* 19 February 1971, p6
75 *Scooter World,* August 1971, p15-22
76 *IOM Courier,* 2 July 1971, p3
77 *Club and Circuit,* No 36, November 1972, p3
78 *Jet Set,* September 1973, p9
79 *Classic Scooterist Scene,* April/May 2012, p30
80 *Scooter and Scooterist,* issue 11 p 2-3
81 *Scooter and Scooterist,* p20
82 *Scooter and Scooterist,* issue 25, p19
83 *Scooter and Scooterist,* issue 25, p22
84 *Scooter and Scooterist,* September 1976, p15
85 *Scooter and Scooterist,* September 1976, p16-17
86 *Scooter and Scooterist,* September 1976, p19
87 *IOM Weekly Times,* 1 September 1981, p1

Acknowledgements

Thank you to everyone who shared their images and memories, and to Terry Cringle for publicising my research in the Isle of Man Examiner and encouraging people to contribute. Special thanks go to Norrie Kerr, for responding to endless requests for information, Les Moore for helping with historical accuracy, John and Mark Kelly from the Isle of Man Scooter Club, and lastly James Cain, for helping me with a biographical history of his father.

Photographic acknowledgements are identified by initials, as follows –

Manx National Heritage (MNH) [to access quote library reference PG/13633]: annotations all by Norrie Kerr
Norrie Kerr (NK)
Norman Ronald (NR)

Keig Collection (Keig) courtesy Lily Publications)
Terry Moore (TM)
Malcolm Black (MB)
Norman Moore (NM)
Les Moore (LM)
Noel Howarth (NH)
Kenny Radcliffe (KR)
Pauline Hewitt (nee Crooks) (PH)
Martin Crooks (PH)
Maureen Cubbon (nee Shegog) (MC)
Eddie Corkill (EC)
Isle of Man Scooter Club (IOMSC)

Steve Jackson
St Johns, Isle of Man

Publisher's note
The contemporary images used within *SCOOTER MANIA!* have come from many sources and, in some instances, are not of the best quality. Nevertheless, because of their importance and relevance to this book, they have been included in order to tell the whole story.

Introduction

When I took up my position within the library and archives at the Manx Museum, I gradually became aware of the huge amount of Manx press coverage given to the Scooter Rally in the late fifties and early sixties, and began to record it. In March 2011, Manx National Heritage launched a new resource, iMuseum (www.imuseum.im), which includes a digitized newspaper database of all the Manx newspapers dating from 1792 to 1960, with some issues of *Holiday News* up to 1966. An advanced search for 'Scooter Rally' returned 622 hits, demonstrating the popularity of what was a huge event in the history of Manx motorsport and tourism.

My next task was to wade through every column inch of newspaper between 1961 and 1976, by means of a digital microfilm scanner in the museum library. Over the coming months, several people came forward and shared their personal experiences and photographs of the Rally. The Manx Press Pictures collection, held within the museum's photographic archives, unearthed many images that can now be seen in their original quality. Rally reports have been sourced from period scooter magazines, enabling me to cover every year in some detail, giving the results and awards for the main competitions.

Steve Jackson

 Manx National Heritage
Eiraght Ashoonagh Vannin

Forewords

BY NORRIE KERR AND MAU SPENCER

To any scooterist who rode their scooter during the late '50s, into the '60s and '70s, the Isle of Man is of special significance. The Holiday Week for Scooterists [another name used for the event] was championed by the Manx Tourist Board, but little did it know how successful its promotion would be ...

From 1957 to 1976 (except 1966 when the event was cancelled due to the seamen's strike) the holiday week gave thousands of scooterists a week of fun, games, competition and socialising.

Having visited and competed on the Isle of Man for many years, I fell in love with the event, the people, and the island. It was a special place, a mecca for scooterists. To this day, I have never forgotten the wonderful weeks spent on the Isle of Man.

This book is a picture window of what went on during the Manx holiday week. It lists the many aspects of what made up the week; reveals how easy it was to make new friends during those seven days, and includes the efforts made to continue this essential scooter event.

I am delighted to have been helpful, in some small way, in the preparation of this vital historic book: a work which not only informs about events of days gone by but which analyses them, too – events which many of today's scooterists will feel envious of.

Steve Jackson has been fervent in his efforts to ensure accuracy and detail in this essential read. He is to be congratulated on his efforts. Read on and enjoy.

Norrie Kerr
Vespa enthusiast and regular Isle of Man competitor

Closed road racing and other sporting activities have forged a unique niche in the history of scootering. Up until now, there has never been a comprehensive, detailed account of those halcyon days on the Isle of Man, when bonds were formed between scooterists over their love of scooter sport.

Working for Manx National Heritage puts Steve Jackson, the author of this long overdue book, in the unique position of being able to plug this gap in scooterist history. The editorial detail and pictorial content of Steve's book is unlikely ever to be bettered.

Mau Spencer
Editor
Classic Scooterist magazine

Chapter 1

The first post-war scooter rally is believed to have taken place in 1948; essentially a camping trip in France organised by the Corgi Club. The scooter boom of the early 1950s led to the formation of several clubs, openly encouraged by Italian scooter manufacturers. In 1952, Vespa held a rally in Bristol, followed by a national rally in Brighton the year after. In 1955, Lambretta clubs staged their first rally, by which time rallies in all of the main towns and cities of the UK had become regular events.

The idea of an Isle of Man Scooter Rally first appeared in the *Isle of Man Examiner* on 26 October, 1956. Mr J M Cain, candidate for East Douglas in the forthcoming election, made the suggestion, along with that of deferring TT week until later in June, and setting up a commission to assess travel to and from the island, with a view to increasing the number of visitors. He believed that a scooter rally would be a big attraction because of the opportunity it would provide to compete over the TT course, and thus bring two full weeks of trade for the island's businesses. Cain also suggested reviving the Highland Gathering, which had been successful before the war, and coincided with the Glasgow Fair holidays in July. This event featured athletic competitions, and was preceded by a pageant, which included dancing and a pipe band.

James Mylchreest Cain was born in 1893, the

Tourist Board publicity shot from the 1957 official programme. (MNH)

youngest of four sons, and was educated at Castletown Grammar School and King William's College, which he left in 1913. In 1914, he joined the Isle of Man Volunteers, before joining the 8th Battalion Lincolnshire Regiment in 1917, shortly after which he was posted to France with the British Expeditionary Force, and was severely wounded leading his platoon 'over the top' on the second day in the major offensive of Passchendaele. Cain was evacuated from France, and, after a long period of convalescence, returned to the island to take up farming with his father and brothers, during which time he met his wife, Jenny (Jean) Crookhall.

During WW2, Cain joined the First Battalion of the Isle of Man Home Guard in 1940, and was appointed Staff Captain in 1943. When the Home Guard was abolished in 1957, he had attained the rank of Lieutenant Colonel, and was awarded the military OBE for his services. Throughout the 1940s and '50s he became a well-known businessman and politician, and was duly elected as a member of the House of Keys (Manx Parliament) in 1956.

Over the coming months, preparations were made to launch an event that – with the exception of 1966 – was to run for the next twenty years. On March 29, 1957, the front page of the *Examiner* reported that the island was to stage a national motor scooter rally at Whitsun, June 8-10, the week immediately following the Golden Jubilee TT, and that this was to be an annual event. It was predicted that the rally would be the biggest of its kind ever staged in the British Isles. A 'Grand Scooter Ball' with special competitions was arranged for the Saturday evening, amidst three days of non-stop entertainment, ranging from reliability tests around the TT course, to treasure hunts, gymkhanas, and a Concours d'Elegance, with £250 prize money to be paid in premium bonds. Scooterists would also pay reduced rates for the sea crossing (later to provoke controversy amongst the motorcycling fraternity).

Mr Charles Fothergill, publicity officer for the Golden Jubilee TT, was tasked with the preliminary organisation – contacting all of the scooter clubs – and reported that there had been considerable interest from the motor trade. The rally also made the front page of the *Isle of Man Times*, published on the same date, where visitors to the forthcoming attraction were described as "scooter pioneers," and the hope was expressed that, although the rally was designed to appeal to a new and different two-wheeled 'public,' it was expected to be "equally as successful and, it is hoped, as long-lived as the TT races." The paper also claimed that a scootering event of this magnitude had never before been experienced in the UK, and urged people to "come abroad to the Isle of Man … because during the rally the island will be yours."

All competitors were to receive a special allocation of fuel permitting 200 miles of coupon-free scootering, but the reduced rates offered to visitors were not welcomed by all. Cyril Quantrill, writing in the current issue of *Motor Cycle News*, claimed that the IOM Tourist Board had "sat on a wasps' nest," and that unless competitors in the Jubilee TT races received the same concessions they were likely to "begin buzzing angrily."[1] Earlier that month, the Tourist Board estimated that an increase in expenditure would be required for 1957, and put the cost of the motor scooter rally at £500.[2] The *Ramsey Courier* predicted that in the region of 250 scooter owners would be visiting the island, and stated that the Tourist Board had arranged the programme in collaboration with Mr T French, secretary of the British Lambretta Club, and Mr C Fothergill.[3]

Visitors were due to arrive on the Friday midnight boats or on Saturday morning, with a treasure hunt taking place in the afternoon. A civic reception, held by the Mayor of Douglas, Councillor W B Kaneen, at the Villa Marina was scheduled for the evening. On Sunday morning, competitors were to assemble at the Victoria Pier arcade to receive an official welcome by the Mayor, who would receive messages of goodwill from English towns. The ceremony was to be followed by a grand parade along the promenade, and then on to Noble's Park for preliminary judging of the Concours d'Elegance. The next event would be a reliability trial around the TT course, with competitors setting off in pairs. Other events included a slow scooter race, a ladies' race, and an up-and-down plank race.

The finals and judging of these events were arranged for Whit Monday, with two special competitions for a Loving Cup (best couple), and the title of 'Scooter Girl.' Male competitors could enter for the title of 'Scooter King of 1957.' Local riders were also urged to attend, and by way of encouragement, a trophy and other prizes were to be offered for the best-performing Manx entrant, with Manx riders also eligible for prizes in the open classes. It was hoped that a permanent organisation would be formed as a parent body in the island to take responsibility for the promotion of future national scooter events. It was claimed that, although scooter clubs existed in some parts of England, there was not yet a parent body in the British Isles, and that the Island rally was in the nature of a pioneer event on a national scale.[4]

The *Isle of Man Weekly Times* also picked up on the fact that scooterists had no motoring organisation behind them, and that the Isle of Man Rally Committee had been formed to organise the events and overcome any and all difficulties encountered. As further incentive to local

SCOOTERMANIA!

entrants, a cup replica and £5 in premium savings bonds would be awarded to the local competitor, male or female, who secured the most marks in the various classes of the rally. It was also reported by the *Peel City Guardian* that this was the "Isle of Man National Championship," open to all competitors from the island.

Prizes for events were listed as follows: Scooter King of Europe: Rose Bowl and £20; Scooter Queen of Europe: Rose Bowl replica and £20; IOM National Championship: cup replica and £5; team with best total marks: trophy and replica (scooter and three-wheeler), and £12. Teams were to consist of four members – male, female or mixed – with the highest three marks gained by the four comprising the final aggregate. Individual prizes were given for the treasure hunt, Concours d'Elegance, and the competitive events, including a one-week Isle of Man holiday with first class steam packet travel for the 'Scooter Girl' winner.[5]

Strong winds and rain prevailed on the Saturday, deterring many of the competitors from reporting to the TT grandstand for the official welcome. The first event was the treasure hunt, on a route which went via Quarter Bridge, St Mark's, Eairy Dam, The Round Table, Four Roads, Port St Mary, and along the Shore Road to Castletown, where the riders were directed to Langness. Around a hundred scooterists attended the Mayor's official civic welcome at the Villa Marina, amidst claims of being overshadowed by 670 hockey players who were being received on the occasion of the annual hockey festival.

Competitors were met by the Deputy Mayor at the Victoria Pier arcade early on Sunday morning, who later rode pillion on the chief marshal's Lambretta. Riders proceeded along the promenade en route to Noble's Park, where they were met by the stewards, Messrs Jim Cain, G D Hanson, and Councillor Harold Rowell. The machines competing in the Concours d'Elegance were scrutinised by Mr R D Vaughan Williams. The next event was the reliability trial, where the riders left in pairs, with the field events taking place in the afternoon. On a lighter note, in the gymkhana events, Tom Bowden of Tyneside was allowed to admit defeat with blowing up a balloon that refused to burst. The team event consisted of a plug relay race, whereby each team member had to insert, use and hand back the plug to one of the officiating Boy Scouts. It was soon realised that finger-tightness was sufficient for the 30 yards involved.[5]

Eighteen-year-old Patricia Aldridge from Luton, a member of the Luton Lambretta Club, was proclaimed 'Scooter Queen of 1957.' The 'Scooter King' winner was P Southall, 20, from Warwick, also a member of his local Lambretta Club, the 'King' and 'Queen' being those competitors with the best total marks from every other

Joan Steele, winner of the 1957 Isle of Man National Championship Award. (IOMSC)

event. Winner of the Isle of Man National Championship was Mrs Joan Steele, of 14, Derby Road, Douglas, and the other premier award – the team prize – was awarded to the Warwickshire Lambretta Club. The Loving Cup – judged by the editors of the four Manx papers: the *Ramsey Courier*, the *Examiner, Mona's Herald* and the *Times* – was awarded to scooter salesman and woman Mr and Mrs K Walker from Liverpool. There were 12 entries for the Scooter Girl contest, and the lucky winner and recipient of the holiday prize was 21-year-old office clerk Marianne Foster from Coventry.

The Lieutenant Governor, Sir Ambrose Flux Dundas, proclaimed himself delighted with the success of the rally, and hoped that competitors would return the following year. He thanked everyone who had helped make the rally a success.

The *Mona's Herald* reported that the organisers had every reason to be satisfied with the island's first scooter rally. Competitors departed after the prize giving, many heading to a similar event in St Albans scheduled to open with an entry of 1500 riders. The paper noted that these "small and stylish machines, with their small petrol consumption, are rapidly growing in popularity, and it is hoped to make this an annual rally in the island's summer calendar."[7]

Chapter 2

1958: FIRST ISLE OF MAN INTERNATIONAL MOTOR SCOOTER RALLY

The 1958 event was discussed at a meeting of the Tourist Board's Race Committee, and in view of the popularity of the initial rally, it was decided to extend the programme to a week instead of three days, a first in Britain as week-long rallies had only ever been held on the continent: it was proposed that the organisation of these events be investigated in order to run the Isle of Man rally along similar lines. The events of 1957 would be repeated, commencing on Saturday with an assembly and get-together in the evening; a 'Ladies' Day' was to be arranged for the Wednesday, and finals of the field events completed on the Friday, at which there would be performances by a scooter display team. A presentation ball and prize giving would conclude the event later that evening. Dates for the second rally were given as June 8-14, with a greater turnout anticipated.[8]

An editorial in the *Examiner*, quoting from *Trader* magazine, recognised the benefit that the rally would bring to the island, and to its retail trade, and urged the Auto Cycle Union to help more with scootering events, despite its heavy TT commitments, in view of the absence of a separate national scooter organisation. The paper went as far as suggesting: "Could the ACU, the island authorities, and the retail motorcycle trade combine to make the annual scooter rally to Douglas the equivalent of the Monte Carlo car rally, with controls at mainland depots (including Liverpool)? A road rally of this nature would be better for the future of pleasure scootering (and for the trade) than the ill-conceived notions of some enthusiasts who are already advocating for next year that scooter races, too, should be held around the TT course."[9]

The next pressing issue was the formation of a Manx scooter club. On August 9, 1957, Mr Edgar Cottier, events organiser for the Tourist Board, and Mr Jim Cain, chairman of the scooter rally sub-committee, left the island to attend rallies in Germany and Austria, staged in Düsseldorf and Salzburg by the respective Vespa clubs.

A meeting was scheduled between Messrs Cottier and Cain and the rally organisers, in order for them to gain insight and advice about staging such large-scale events. It was also announced that a Lambretta scooter was being displayed in the window of the Tourist Board offices in Victoria Street, along with a publicity display for the 1958 event. Mr Cottier claimed this had attracted a lot of interest from visitors, and that many scooterists had called in, several of whom had attended the rally, and had returned to the island for a holiday: all of these received promises of support for the following year's event.

The trip to Germany and Austria was hailed a success, prompting the promoters of the 1958 scooter rally to consider launching an international event, in order to attract entries from the continent. "We first went to Düsseldorf, which turned out to be quite a big affair." Mr Cottier said. "Some 800 motor-scooterists took part, whilst no fewer than 1200 people attended the dinner and ball that followed. This was a successfully-run social event in connection with the rally, and, apart from the presentation of prizes, there was also a cabaret provided by a troupe of acrobatic dancers."[10]

During their stay in Düsseldorf, the island 'ambassadors' met the presidents of the Vespa clubs of Germany and Holland, the president of the Lambretta Club of Düsseldorf and Westphalia, and the secretary-general of the Dutch Vespa Club. Mr Cottier stated that the officials they consulted showed considerable interest in Manx proposals, and were to consider sending over teams to compete.

At Fuschi, near Salzburg, the Manx visitors attended a smaller rally which, although more of a gathering due to the absence of sporting events, several countries were nevertheless represented. They were also told that there were far too many small rallies on the continent, which were held to the detriment of each other. The continental officials stated their preference for three or four major

L-R: Graham Oates, Edgar Cottier and Harold Rowell prepare for the 1958 rally. (MNH)

European rallies, as was the case with competitive motorcycling. The continental clubs requested the Isle of Man's definitive plan for the next rally as soon as possible in order to consider arrangements for attending, prompting the sub-committee to meet and draw up a provisional programme. One of the proposals brought home to the island was that there should be a 24-hour 'Le Mans-type' event during the week – a reliability test with two riders per machine.[11]

A meeting was held in the Tynwald Committee Rooms on September 18 to discuss the formation of a Manx Scooter Club, with all interested parties invited to attend. Edgar Cottier estimated there were already nearly 200 scooter owners on the island. He had recently visited Morecambe Scooter Rally with councillor Harold Rowell, and they were amazed at the number of scooterists who were displaying pennants from the 1957 Manx Rally.

It had already been decided that the following year's event would be known as the 'Isle of Man International Motor Scooter Rally.'[12] Plans were completed in September 1957, and after the assembly at Victoria Pier on Sunday June 8, competitors were to partake in a grand parade of honour along Douglas promenade to the TT grandstand. The highlight of the rally – when competitors in the 24-hour reliability run around the TT course would be despatched – would commence at 12 noon on Tuesday. Testing of the TT course took place the night the clocks went back in order to set average speeds for the reliability trials, due to take place at the forthcoming

Manx International Rally. Participants included Graham Oates (Scottish Six Days Gold Star and first class award winner); Councillor Rowell (Triple Scottish Six Days Trial award winner and former Manx Grand Prix competitor); Edgar Cottier (Tourist Board and rally committee); Mr Jeff Shimmin (official timekeeper); Guy Reid (brother-in-law of Geoff Duke); Neil Kelly (Captain of the Peveril Motor Cycle Club), and Stan Wardell and Bertie Rowell, who were responsible for time checks.

Testing began at 4pm on Saturday, October 5, and continued throughout the night until 4am the following morning. Harold Rowell put in 16 laps on his Lambretta 150, making a total mileage of 1000 (1609km) over a three-week period, taking into account his recent participation in the Morecambe Scooter Rally. The findings of these experimental tests were later reported to the rally organising committee in preparation for the following year's event.

As plans for the rally gained momentum, foreign interest continued. The Isle of Man International Motor Scooter Rally Committee received a letter from the chairman of the Pietermaritzburg Club, seeking advice about organising a similar event in South Africa. He stated that motor scooter riding was new to South Africa, but had quickly become very popular. In January 1958, an article about the Isle of Man Rally was printed in the Dutch publication *Scooter,* and the Tourist Board received two inquiries from Holland regarding possible entries, one of which came from the Hague Vespa Club. The rally also came to the notice of the BBC, which expressed its hope of showing a film of the Isle of Man in the new year, and pledged that sporting events "such as the TT races, cycle races, the Manx Grand Prix Races, and the scooter rally would all receive excellent coverage."[13] As the year progressed, international interest continued. Eight weeks prior to the rally, there were 40 entries, with the organisers confirming that many more were on their way, including parties from France and Holland.

Regulations were issued at the end of January for the 24-hour test over the TT course, due to take place on June 10-11. Two riders were to be nominated for each scooter, taking turns to ride, and a non-riding manager to assist refuelling was also named. In addition to the individual award, there would be a team event with four scooters per team. Four classes of scooter were eligible for the test: up to 100cc, 101-150cc, 151-200cc, and scooters in excess of 200cc. The largest machines were set to cover 20 laps of the course (755 miles/1215km) in 12 hours, at an average of 31.4mph (50.53kph). The second category was designated 29 laps at 29.8mph (47.96kph); the third 18 laps at 28.3mph (45.54kph), and

Harold Rowell (right) with Eric Brockway, MD of Douglas Motorcycles, importer of Vespa scooters to the UK (left), and Derek Guy, secretary of the British Lambretta Owners Association, in a Tourist Board publicity shot, March 1958. (MNH)

organising committee was turning into the scootering equivalent of the ACU with regard to its national rally. Two days before the final entry date, 103 machines had been entered, an increase of 50 over the previous year. It was also announced that there would be one week's grace for late entries, albeit at double the entry fee.[15] Prizes and trophies were arriving from a number of companies to accompany the two silver cups already presented to the Tourist Board by Slazenger. Double Diamond contributed the Scooter Rally Cup. A new trophy, the 'Watsonian Cup,' for the best performing sidecar outfit, would be presented by Mr Ron Watson.

Freddie Frith OBE, a former Grand Prix motorcycle road racing World Champion, was to represent a Lambretta Owner's Association team in the 24-hour reliability trial over the mountain circuit, with Bernard Howard as co-driver. An entry was also received from Denis Parkinson: triple winner of the Manx Grand Prix. One of the last entrants was Herr Luzien Schwoerer, a German rider from Düsseldorf who claimed to be the oldest scooterist in Germany. Another late entry was received by cablegram from Oslo, bringing the entry list to 180 machines and 240 riders.

Further testing of the TT course took place in March 1958, but on this occasion Harold Rowell was accompanied by Derek Guy of the British Lambretta Owner's Association. Mr Guy arrived on the island with A Kimber, Lambretta's competition manager for the rally. Mr Guy claimed that it was a difficult course, but well within the capabilities of the Lambretta. It was discovered that a newsletter had been distributed to 25,000 members, and that 107 clubs had been issued with IOM guides and accommodation details. On April 26, the *Green Final* reported that letters had been pouring in from England, Ireland, South Africa, Bombay, Sweden and Holland, and, furthermore, there was a possibility of television coverage for the TT reliability test. The *Mona's Herald* also claimed there was a likelihood of a team from Italy, and an inquiry had been received from the German city of Bonn.[16]

The rally opened on Sunday, June 8, bringing a cavalcade of colour to Douglas. Crowds were out along the promenade from Victoria Pier to Summerhill to witness the long line of visitors from Britain and countries overseas, including the German entrant, Luzian Schwoerer. The front of his scooter was emblazoned with

the smallest machines 16 laps at 25.2mph (40.55kph). Any scooter fitted with a sidecar was to compete in the class with the next lower engine capacity.

It was specified that the event would take place on the open road, and that entrants would have to comply with the Highway Code. Marks would be lost for being more than five minutes early or more than one minute late at any control point, with times taken at the start of every lap. No rider was to ride for more than eight consecutive hours without rest; pacing was to be barred, and replenishment of fuel was to be done at the official depot only. It was claimed that "The TT course regularity test would be a highlight of the 1958 scooter rally, and being the first scooter event of its kind may – as with the TT – form the pattern for all future events of this type throughout the world."[14]

The publication *Motor Cycle* considered that, with the right publicity, the scooter rally could hardly fail to generate enthusiasm, despite its claim that the inaugural rally of 1957 had been a "disappointment," and that the

continued page 16

Top left: Deputy Mayor of Douglas in
the Vespa rickshaw leads the convoy.
(Keig Collection: courtesy
Lily Publications)

Far left: 1958 Concours d'Elegance
winner, Joan Steele. (IOMSC)

Left: Herr Luzian Schwoerer.
(Keig Collection: courtesy
Lily Publications)

Above: Bradford 52 Vespa Club.
(Keig Collection: courtesy
Lily Publications)

Right: View of the pit lane.
(Keig Collection: courtesy
Lily Publications)

the badges of clubs from the many places he had visited during his scootering career, over which he had clocked up 100,000 miles (160,934km) on his Vespa. One of the pennants displayed on his machine was a 'superstitious 13,' decorated with skull and crossbones. Vespa riders emerged from their hotels in bright yellow overalls; their Lambretta rivals dressed in royal blue. The Deputy Mayor of Douglas took his seat in a Vespa rickshaw to lead the convoy to the TT grandstand in Glencrutchery Road. A short religious service was conducted by the Reverend R H Reid in the TT examination tent near to the grandstand, before riders conducted start, acceleration, and stop tests in the pit lane.

An elimination inspection for the Concours d'Elegance competition took place shortly afterwards. Two Vespa-riding entrants were Mr and Mrs R Siddell from Bradford, celebrating their 25th wedding anniversary (their honeymoon had been spent in Douglas). Mrs Siddell was the secretary of the Vespa Club of Bradford, and was entered to ride for Great Britain in the forthcoming International Vespa Rally.

The opening parade brought with it the first sign of rain, which cleared a little in the afternoon for a one-lap reliability run around the TT course, punctuated by four tests at secret control points. At the straight-line stop in Ramsey Square, a crowd of 200 spectators amassed to watch proceedings. Monday morning and afternoon the preliminary and eliminating heats of the field events took place in Noble's Park, where large crowds gathered to watch events such as the plank race. The weather held throughout the morning, although afternoon riders were not as fortunate. Early that evening the scooters congregated on the promenade to travel in convoy to Peel, although many were deterred by worsening weather conditions.

The 24-hour regularity test began at noon on Monday, as riders and co-riders were dispatched from the grandstand on to the TT course. With the course reaching 1000ft (305m) on the mountain section, visibility was seriously compromised by fog and mist. Several of the pits were manned by works teams, including Puch, Maicoletta and Peugeot, and at 9pm that evening, 43 extra riders joined the fray to begin the 12-hour regularity test, billed as a "gruelling test" by the *Isle of Man Daily Times*, with one rider per machine riding for twelve hours without rest.

Riders were flagged off by the Mayor of Douglas, Councillor J R Killip, JP, in sight of around 800 spectators. Riders in the 12-hour event occupied the right-hand side of the road, with the left reserved for riders in the 24-hour event, some of whom had already been riding for nine hours: if a change of rider was scheduled, they were directed into the pits. British-made scooters scored a resounding success in the 12- and 24-hour reliability trials on the team prize board; four Manx riders won the junior event team award. Manx Grand Prix (MGP) and TT rider Jackie Wood, MGP rider Colin Broughton, George Gelling and Reuben Hardy, an entrant in the Southern 100 races, George Kewley and Noel Howarth all won first class awards in the 12-hour regularity test. Local riders also included Miss A A Corlett, Guy Reid, Dennis Craine, and A Quayle, who was forced to retire his Swallow Gadabout on lap three with ignition trouble. A columnist for the *IOM Daily Times* reported that Noel's Moby machine, purchased the previous year, was not given the "full treatment" that many of the scooters were by mechanics brought over by manufacturers' teams. Speaking in 2012, Noel shared with me memories of this event, and the following statement is written in his own words:[17]

"The weather conditions for the 12-hour night regularity test were atrocious, with thick mist as low as the Tower Bends at Ramsey and Bedstead, Douglas. I rode a Motobecane Moby 125cc which my father had 'souped up.' Motobecane was completely disinterested in any form of sponsorship, but after my small success, wanted to use me in advertising promotions, which I refused in typical Anglo Saxon language, in response to its earlier rejection. My hazy memory does not recall the 12-hour test as a regularity test as my overriding memories are of riding at full throttle all the time, treating it like a race – I do not recall observing speed limits or checking in anywhere on the circuit. I do remember many times when over-revving the engine (down Bray Hill, for example) I hoped the cylinder would not propel itself through the seat!

"Once round the Hairpin one entered thick mist, and visibility was reduced to the distance of two white centre road markings. This situation continued until Bedstead. Of course, this caused problems as one would suddenly arrive behind slower scooters and violent avoiding action had to be taken. This I remember well as I charged through the mist at speeds well exceeding any safety limits, but I knew the mountain section well. The only shock I got was when four green lights appeared in front of me so rapidly I had no time to react, and drove through the middle of them, only to glimpse that they were sheep – the green light puzzle was answered – it was their eyes.

"During the period of 12 hours my father, Jack Howarth, acted as my pit manager, and kept a time on me so that on a refuelling stop he could have a hot mug (tin) of coffee for me, which, to keep me warm, he laced with a goodly slug of Lambs Dark Rum. It was only when the event was over that I realised I had emptied the bottle – I must have been quite sozzled during the night as I did not even drink in those days – no wonder I took so many risks. I recall a dice with Andre Baldet [on a Vespa 150cc] who I would overtake on the mountain in the mist but who would pass me just after Creg ny Baa. On the last lap I was determined to get to the grandstand ahead of him. I huddled down as low as I could get, going like the 'clappers' from the Creg, and somehow managed to do so. This was the only event I entered as I could not afford to damage my scooter in the 'motocross' type of events, whereas the works teams could afford to do so."

The Bond Scooter Club and British Lambretta Owners Association 150 team completed the test without loss of marks, but the winning team in the 12-hour event was the Alpine Aces (Puch). Riders had reported appalling conditions on the mountain, with reduced visibility caused by a blanket of mist and pouring rain from above the Gooseneck down to Hillberry. Lena Mangan fell off at Brandish, necessitating an unscheduled pit stop at 5am. Headlight failure caused Henry Kissack in total darkness to crash into a bank up on the mountain, inflicting minor injuries. A third accident befell Mrs Bethune-Pierce, who was dismounted at Governor's Bridge at the end of her third lap. Despite loosening a tooth and facial cuts, she carried on for another lap before retiring.[18]

On Wednesday evening, the final heats were held for the field events, but fading light meant that a couple of them were delayed until Thursday, in order to facilitate a daring exhibition from the Thames Valley Vespa Display Team.

Thursday evening played host to the point-to-point competition, held in a pasture behind the grandstand. It was a scramble-type course circling two rough meadows, where a gap in the hedge took riders across banks and ditches. Described by *Motor Cycling* magazine as a "rough course with awkward jumps," J Hornsby (Lambretta) broke his leg in a practice session, with many riders scratching their entry. D Palmer was the favourite for the final, having won his heat with an impressive handling display. With half the race completed, he held a near-half lap lead over Dennis Christian (Vespa) when he was foiled by a blocked air filter, allowing Dennis to romp to victory.[19]

The rally was hailed a great success, although it was hoped that more foreign competitors would compete in 1959, given the interest generated by this year's event. At the presentation awards held at the Palace Ballroom on the Friday evening, Lieutenant Governor Dundas was introduced by Mr Jim Cain, who thanked scooter enthusiasts for their participation, and paid tribute to the hard work of the organising committee. Overall champion and winner of the National Scooter Rose Bowl and Motor Cycling Award, and the Belstaff Trophy for

Noel Howarth in light overalls, second right, competing in the 12-hour regularity test. (NH)

Thames Valley Vespa Display Team, (Keig Collection: courtesy Lily Publications)

Best Male Performance of the First International Rally, was Mr I T V Smith (Maico). Joan Steele (Lambretta) was crowned Scooter Queen and overall female champion, and awarded the Power and Pedal Rose Bowl. She was also declared Scooter Girl of the rally and winner of the Concours d'Elegance for the pre-1958 class.

Other awards went to Andre Baldet (Vespa), Concours d'Elegance in the 1958 class; Dennis Christian (Vespa), Wallace Trophy for best Manx performance, and the Watsonian Trophy for best sidecar performance, plus Harold Day (DKR) won a trophy for best performance on a British scooter.

The Thames Valley Vespa Club, with 14 machines,

Lieutenant Governor Dundas presents Joan Steele with the Concours d'Elegance trophy. (IOMSC)

Peter Agg chats with TT ace Freddie Frith. (Keig Collection: courtesy Lily Publications)

covered a total of 3091 miles (4974km) to the assembly point, and won the National Assembly Award (the Double Diamond Trophy). This class was open to clubs and groups in England, Scotland and Ireland, and group mileage was based on the distance covered by members, multiplied by the machines in the group. P J Grove, M Scanlon and T C Behan of Thames Valley won the Best Team Award, and the Scooter and Three-Wheeler Shield. The South Devon Vespa Club received a special commendation for covering 3084 miles (4963km) on eleven machines. Luzian Schwoerer from Germany was

presented with the Vespa Trophy for "most meritorious performance," and also won the individual award for the Assembly Rally.

A special award was presented to J O Oosterling, who had covered the journey from Limbury in Holland on his Zundapp Bella, and the Loving Cup competition – judged by band leader Ken Mackintosh and *Motor Cycling's* Norman Sharpe – was won by Joan Steele and her partner, W Toms. TT star Freddie Frith claimed he had "thoroughly enjoyed" his re-acquaintance with the TT course, on what was his first visit to the island since his retirement from motorcycle racing in 1949.

The director for Lambretta Concessionaires, Peter Agg, praised the event in a letter published in the *IOM Times* on June 20, 1958, and stated that everyone at Lambretta hoped that the island's sponsorship of the scooter rally would be a long one. *Motor Cycle and Cycle Trader* urged the authorities to concentrate on the 12- and 24-hour regularity tests and omit the field events,

Right: John and Pat Kelly (nee Garrett) pictured opposite the marine biological station, showing Bradda Head in the background. Tourist Board publicity shot. (MNH)

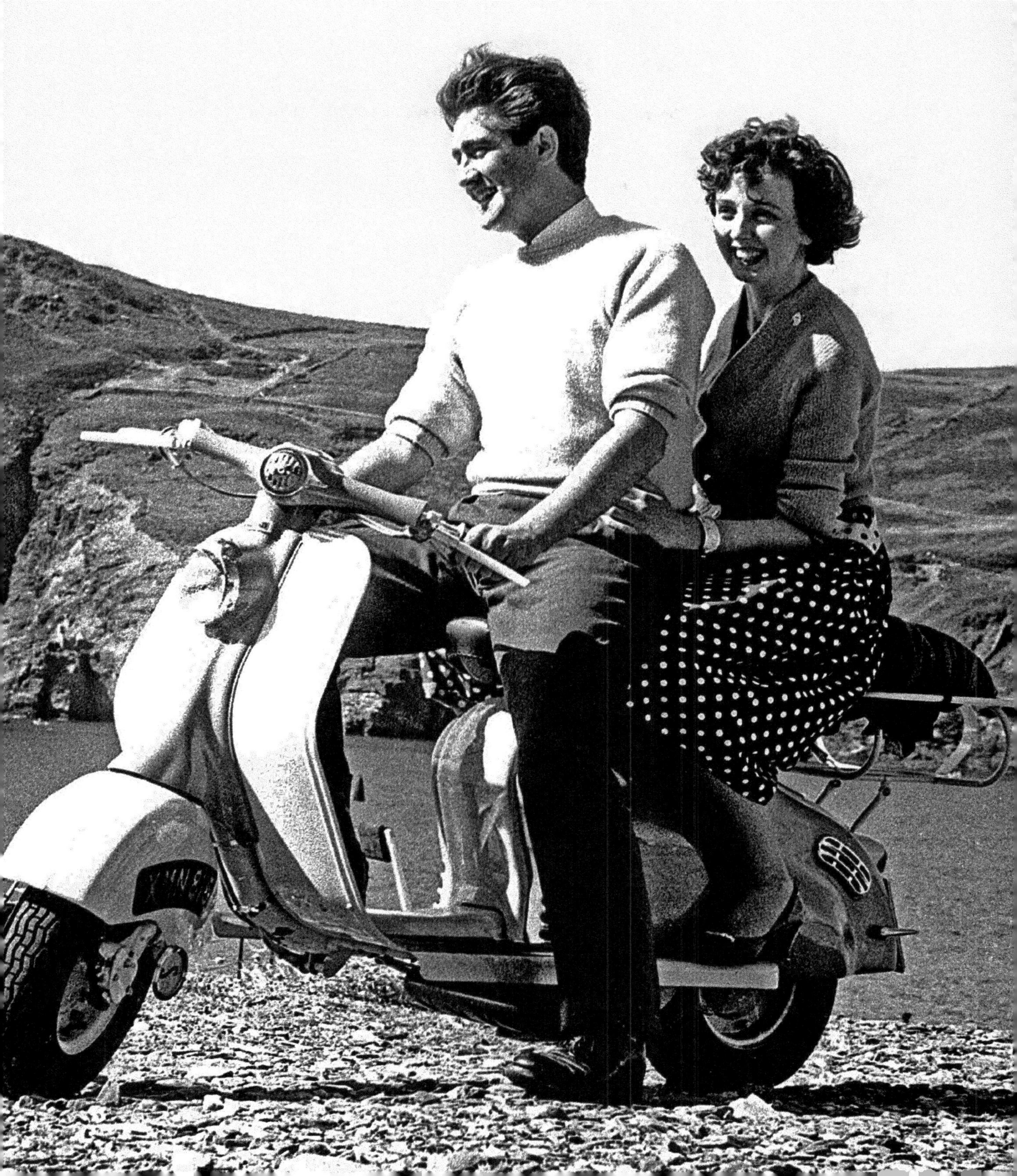

Frenchman Andre Baldet and Manxman Dennis Christian completed 100 laps of the TT course. (IOMSC)

claiming that "cavorting with scooters on see-saws and circling bumpy courses are activities for specialists." It was suggested that the activities held on the TT course, together with the island's scenery, were the event's trump cards, rather than field sports that could be played anywhere, and that with more "spirited and imaginative preparation, and greater co-operation from the industry and trade," the Isle of Man Scooter Rally could become the leading event of its type in Europe.[20]

The 1958 event was highlighted in one of four 16mm colour films, made available from the Castrol library to loan to motorcycle clubs. The film – *Two Wheel Trio* – portrayed three widely-contrasting events: the Cotswold Cup trial run in a March snow storm; the Italian motocross Grand Prix, and the Isle of Man Rally.

Lambretta responded to the rally's success by announcing its involvement with a new venture entitled Lambretta Hire (Isle of Man) Service, recently installed in the former *Examiner* building in Douglas. On July 4, 1958, the front page of the *Isle of Man Weekly Times* revealed that 30 brand new Lambrettas were to arrive that same day, dubbed 'L-Day for the island,' via the steam packet. An appeal had been made for young enthusiasts to model the new machines at various points around the island over the weekend, and parades were organized along all the promenades in the hope that young people would take to the streets on this modern form of transport. It was claimed that L-Day for the island would enable visitors to enjoy their stay more fully and economically than before.

The scooter rally – which had "blazed the trail" for bigger and better rallies in the future – was the catalyst for the venture. However, not everyone was quite as enthusiastic about the photo opportunity. MNH library manager Paul Weatherall was contacted in 2013 by a relative of a couple pictured at Bradda Head. Pat Garrett and John Kelly had their pictures taken on the Lambretta quite by chance: they had gone down to Port Erin with some friends, riding on John's racing Norton. They were approached by Bill Peters, the well-known photographer, with whom they were acquainted, and asked if they would pose on the scooter. They knew nothing about the appeal for models, didn't get paid for doing it, and got a lot of stick from their biking friends, especially when one of the shots was used by Lambretta at a bike show at Olympia in London, and seen by friends of Pat and John who went to the show. The negatives of the publicity pictures taken for this event are held in the Manx Museum Reading Room.

Moves were now under way to bring all scooter clubs under the aegis of a National Scooter Council, administered by the Auto Cycle Union, and proposals were drawn up by an ACU executive, Mr J McNulty, and Mr Brian Keyes, representative of the North London Lambretta Club. It was reported that, in the draft constitution, there was provision for all scooter events to come under the Union's general competition rules, and that this could lead to elimination of Tourist Board control of the IOM event. It was suggested that this could be circumvented by the board taking the "bold step" of forming an International Scooter Union,[21] with headquarters in the island. It was noted that the non-affiliation of Lambretta and Vespa clubs would weaken any such proposal, and the Tourist Board would do well to obtain their support.

To generate publicity for the scooter rally, Frenchman Andre Baldet and Manxman Dennis Christian completed 100 laps of the TT course in under 100 hours between Monday 18 and Friday 23 August. Despite encountering heavy rain, fog and drizzle, they were still an hour in hand by Friday morning, and despite the ordeal the Vespa GS they used remained in tip-top condition. Andre took to the saddle with Dennis riding pillion for the final lap, finally reaching the finish line at 5.35pm. Amongst the crowd was band leader Ken Mackintosh, who placed victory laurel wreaths around the weary riders. Andre and Dennis were later guests of honour at Fort Anne Hotel.

Chapter 3

1959: ISLE OF MAN SCOOTER CLUB

On Wednesday, 12 November, 1958, the Isle of Man Scooter Club held its annual meeting at the Queens Hotel, chaired by Mr J B Bolton, MHK, who told delegates that the success of the International Scooter Rally would depend on the hard work of scooterists and the island's tourist industry, and that they should follow the example of the devoted band of motorcycling enthusiasts who had made the TT and MGP successful. It was noted that at the end of the club's first year, attendance at club meetings had been poor, despite the club being formed as a result of popular demand. Mr. Bolton decreed that the year had been successful and praised the efforts of the club secretary, Miss Maureen Mackay, who had been a "tower of strength" throughout the year. He urged Manx riders to participate in the rally, pointing out that their success could further promote the island.

Mr Harold Rowell, in moving the adoption of the chairman's report, expressed his appreciation for the work done by the president (Mr J M Cain), and Mr Bolton. In presenting the secretary's report, Miss Mackay regretted that some club events had been poorly supported, but pointed out that a fair number of members had competed in the rally: she paid particular tribute to Miss Corlett and Miss Mangan who had put up fine performances in the 12-hour tests, and Mrs Steel who gained awards in the field events. Officials for the coming year were duly elected, with J M Cain remaining as president, and Edgar Cottier, secretary of the first two rallies, elected vice-president.

The dates of June 6-13 were duly published for the 1959 gathering. The main prizes were to be for road events, with the Concours d'Elegance, Scooter Girl and Loving Cup competitions becoming minor contests, along with the field events. Monte Carlo was again cited as the model for the rally from a number of start points, each of which would be 250 to 300 miles from the final embarkation point.[22] All competitors were to participate in the Sunday morning parade, travelling from a nominated starting point to the grandstand (failure to do this without prior permission from the stewards would incur a penalty), and compete in a one-lap reliability test. It was also declared that in the 24-hour reliability test, the rally competitor must drive for the first 12 hours so that their performance could be judged on a par with riders in the 12-hour event. If there was no outright winner, a speed test could be used to decide the tie. The Isle of Man Scooter Club ruled that a competitor may take part in either the 12- or 24-hour event, but not both, so that an entrant in the '24' could not have his riding for the first 12 hours regarded as entry for the 12-hour test.

In order to promote the International Scooter Rally and the bicycle TT, the Tourist Board acquired a stand at Earls Court, having produced a special publication entitled *Race and Rally*, for circulation throughout England during the coming months. It was estimated that 50,000 copies would be distributed from Earls Court, and by post to the main clubs and travel agents. Mr Cain expressed a desire to draw visitors to all parts of the island for these events, and not just those immediately adjacent to the TT course. He also recognized the need for more volunteers to man all the points created by the rapid expansion of events, and welcomed reinforcements to the small band of existing helpers.[23]

The rally organisers attempted to attract more manufacturer interest for 1959, by inviting 'works' entries and teams to compete for special awards in a category distinct from the general rally. It was proposed that after the 24-hour regularity run, works machines should be placed 'in bond' until the next day, when a Monte Carlo-type test would be held in the mountains, with stop and re-start tests. A full week of competitive and social events was mooted, with a reception ball arranged for the evening of Sunday, June 7.

The first overseas entry was received on 31 March

SCOOTERMANIA!

Rita Hammerton pictured in the June 12, 1959 issue of Holiday News.

Windmill Girl Wins Loving Cup

LOVING CUP WINNERS Rita Hammerton and her passenger, London policeman David Waterman on a Lambretta selected in the finals of the Scooter Rally events at Villa Marina. Douglas on Thursday.

from Mike Walters, a resident of Gwelo in Southern Rhodesia. An inquiry was also received from the Central Auto Club of the USSR, giving the new rally secretary, Pat Callin, a translation dilemma. An appeal for help was placed in the *IOM Daily Times*, which also published news that a Jawa scooter team would be attending from Czechoslovakia, bringing manufacturer teams to twelve.

Jawa was a previous TT entrant, and before the war the famous Brooklands star George Patchett managed its TT team entry.[24] Celebrity entrants included 'Windmill Girls' Wendy Clarke and Rita Hammerton, performers from the Windmill Theatre in London, who were given special leave to compete in the Assembly Rally, the Concours d'Elegance, and the Scooter Girl contest at the Villa Marina as members of the Bromley Innocents Lambretta Club.

By the beginning of June, entrants had exceeded 200 in number, amidst claims that the event would go a long way toward the promoter's dream of a rally that would attract 1000 scootererists, making it the best in Britain. The Assembly Rally had designated starting points in London, Liverpool, Northampton, Newcastle, York and Stirling, and in addition to the usual events was added the 'pathfinders' test' for non-residents, designed to take riders off the island's highways and into the byways. There were 117 entries for the 12-hour event and 73 for the 24-hour classic, with 101 in the one-lap reliability class. A Manx team was organised to participate in the Assembly Rally starting at Liverpool, consisting of Hazel Christian, Jack Woods and Ken Harding; all on 150cc Vespas.

This year's rally also attracted the attention of the BBC, which announced it would be featuring the event on the programme 'World of Sport,' scheduled to air on June 12.[25]

At midnight on Friday, June 5, 150 of the rally entrants gathered at the eight starting points of the Assembly Rally, each close on 250 miles (402km) from the final embarkation point. One of the official timekeepers, Mr E J Shimmin, crossed to Liverpool to send off the 28 Vespa Club riders. 58 individuals finished the course without loss of marks (penalties could be incurred at the various checkpoints for early or late arrival). Colin Broughton of Ramsey rode for the Puch team, whilst another Manxman, Dennis Christian, rode for Vespa. Other Manx competitors in the Assembly Rally included Harold Rowell, Ken Harding, Jackie Wood, Fred Stephen, and Miss Hazel Christian.

In the pits: the NSU team about to set off in the 12-hour regularity test.
(Keig Collection: courtesy Lily Publications)

Riders take a well -earned meal break during the 24-hour event. (Keig Collection: courtesy Lily Publications)

Staff News
● Twenty-year old Maureen Shegog of Douglas branch won an award in the 24-hour reliability trial in the International Motor Scooter Rally. She was one of the four ladies out of a field of seventy three competitors. The trial was held over the famous mountain course in the Isle of Man—nineteen 37-mile laps to be covered at an average

speed of 30 m.p.h. ; and this meant driving at 55 m.p.h. some of the time, no mean feat on a 148 c.c. engine. Maureen drove continuously for the last nine laps and came off once—at the Ramsey hairpin.

● John Munday of Norwich branch has won the men's singles title in the Norfolk County Closed Tennis Championships. He regularly represents the County.

● Joan Mann (Head Office) was selected for the regional finals of the **Miss Secretary of Great Britain, 1959** competition organised by Remington Rand. She is the secretary (and a founder member) of The Private Secretaries' Association, which means she also holds the Private Secretary's Diploma of the London Chamber of Commerce. In 1953 she was seconded from the Bank to act as the secretary to the manager of the New Zealand rugger team in this country. Miss Mann is now Mr. C. H. Wigg's amanuensis.

Do rising prices cause misgiving?
Then smoke "Tom Long" and life's worth living.

THE DARK HORSE
AUGUST 1959

Lloyds Bank staff newsletter, The Dark Horse, 1959.

its scooter patrol girls wearing distinctive uniforms that matched the blue of their Vespas and sidecars. A second steamer arrived later in the afternoon containing the remaining sidecar outfits, and that evening a number of competitors attended the reception dance at the Villa Marina, as guests of the Mayor and Town Council.

Corporation staff were employed to fit out the pits in the grandstand for the 12- and 24-hour events, several of which were allocated to manufacturers, clubs and petroleum firms. Regulations were amended so that average speeds could range between 24.75mph (39.83kmh) and 33mph (53.11kmh), with a one-minute early or late margin (compared to five minutes for the previous year). Crowds amassed in the grandstand and along Glencrutchery Road to watch the scooters roar off one by one toward Bray Hill, led by the bigger capacity machines, reports indicating that spectators were gathered at various vantage points, some remaining even after darkness fell. Strong winds prevailed, especially on the mountain, causing some entrants to be blown off line as they approached Kate's Cottage.

Just after 7am, A C Carr was the first to finish in the 12-hour class, riding a Lambretta. Two riders were admitted to hospital after crashing in separate incidents near Handley's Corner.[26] Windmill Girls Wendy Clarke and Rita Hammerton were amongst the spectators in the pits on Monday evening, having scootered from London to Liverpool on Friday night, arriving just five minutes late at the control point. They competed in the one-lap reliability trial on Sunday, and thought the TT course was "a piece of cake." P Sadler (Phoenix) was the winner of the one-lap reliability test, followed by Harold Rowell (Lambretta) in 2nd place. The Overall Team Award was won by the Thames Valley Vespa Club.

Maureen Cubbon (nee Shegog) recalled the 1959 regularity test during a visit to the Manx Museum in 2012. Dudley, her partner in this event, completed the night shift with ten or 11 laps to Maureen's nine. Maureen pointed out that "calls of nature could be a problem for the girls," but that she had a friend who lived next to the Crosby Hotel, where she was able to visit for a pit stop. The rally was featured in the August edition of Lloyds Bank's staff newsletter, with Maureen pictured refuelling behind the grandstand. The article reported her becoming de-seated at Ramsey Hairpin: an incident which occurred when the rider behind her failed to slow sufficiently. Fortunately, Maureen was able to continue, although the other rider sustained damage and was forced to retire.

Upon arrival in Douglas on Saturday morning, the Harbour Board arranged for a special ramp to assist speedy disembarkation of the scooters, watched by a large crowd waiting at Battery Pier, with television cameras on stand-by to record the scene. The RAC and AA were on hand, escorting groups of riders to the rally office, where it was noted that the RAC had sent over

Maureen Shegog and her riding partner, Tommy Jennings, in the Loving Cup competition. (MC)

Manx success was reported for the 24-hour test, with two Puch teams competing in the manufacturer team award class. Manxmen Colin Broughton and George Gelling were co-riders in the Puch number 2 team, dropping just one mark, and thus qualifying for a first class award. The Scooter King winner – who also received the Isle of Man International Scooter Rally Trophy as the premier prize – was R H Jones from Chester, riding his 'Diana' scooter. Two immaculate Vespas claimed the Slazenger trophy replicas, along with £5 in prize money, for the Concours d'Elegance. Mrs E Whittle of the Hitchin Vespa 105 Club won the pre-1959 class, and the 1959 class winner was Didi Baldet, wife of scooter dealer and fellow competitor Andre, himself a first class award winner for the 12-hour regularity test in 1958.

Competitors numbered 85 in the 12-hour event, and 73 in the 24-hour. A total of 25 women competed in the reliability tests, nine of which were Manx locals, including 18-year-old Hazel Christian, who came very close to winning the coveted title of Scooter Queen, awarded to the female rider with the highest number of marks from the Assembly Rally, the Grand Parade, the one-lap TT course regularity test, the 12- or 24-hour regularity test, and the elimination test. When the marks were totalled up on the Thursday evening, Hazel, secretary of the Isle of

The Lambretta no 2 team, which took 2nd place in the Manx 400 team class. (Keig Collection: courtesy Lily Publications)

'Queen for a day' Hazel Christian, featured in the IOM Examiner of June 18, 1959.

Man Vespa Club, was told she would be awarded the title. Twenty-four hours later at the presentation dance, it was explained that a mistake had been made, and that she had missed the title by 12 seconds in the Assembly Rally, losing out to Miss S Simmons of Newcastle. Hazel did, however, carry off a silver replica award for the 12-hour regularity test.

Other Manx success was a second class award in the manufacturers' class which went to Maureen McKay, secretary of the Isle of Man Scooter Club, and co-driver for David Gallagher (Maico); the first woman to ride in a manufacturer's team. Awards were also collected by Sheila Leneghan, Anne Corlett, and Muriel Gelling.[27]

The rally featured in the August issue of *Motorcycle and Cycle Trader*, with feedback coming from Colonel C R Gray, MD of the parent company concerned with Bond scooters. In his précis of the report made to the rally secretary, he stated that "the improvements over previous years' events were very marked, the organisation greatly improved, and the event thoroughly enjoyed by every member of the Bond team." He did, however, include a list of points he thought could further improve the event. His primary concern was the "atrocious" standard of driving, with many riders a "menace to other competitors, as well as themselves." Gray also claimed that mileages in the Assembly Rally were inaccurate; petrol and refreshments were not always available as stated, and no checks existed to ensure that the rider entrant did actually ride in the rally! A suggestion that route cards should be signed at the start, finish, and each checkpoint was duly made.

Colonel Gray insisted that if Bond was to compete again in the '24,' a complete ban of team service vans on the course would have to be implemented, except in the event of serious injury, and that this rule should be enforced by travelling marshals. Praise was given for the organisation of the elimination test, although it was said that this test may be too severe for the average scooterist, prompting the question of whether the rally might become a scooter TT, attracting mostly works-sponsored drivers, or scooterists who were likely to bring the family over for a holiday at the same time?

Many of the points made in Colonel Gray's report concerned the prevention of unfair practices, in order to reduce the number of allegations made at the 1958 event, and he stated that Bond and other teams would not be willing to enter another team in the manufacturer class unless every possible loophole in the regulations was sealed.[28]

QUEEN FOR A DAY

MISS HAZEL CHRISTIAN, 18 years old secretary of the Isle of Man Vespa Club received the news on Thursday night that she had attained the highest number of marks over the week, at the Scooter Rally and was to be awarded the title of Scooter Queen, the supreme award of the rally for women. But disappointment was hers when 24 hours later at the presentation dance it was announced that she had lost the title by a narrow margin.

Further concerns were raised in *Scooter World* magazine, which claimed that "much of the organisation was not up to rally standards. In one event, the regulations were not received until – for some – the event was over. Much uncertainty existed about regulations generally, and, at one point, protests were being voiced thick and fast – not a healthy state of affairs. More than one team manager said 'Never again!' and while some of the accusations were a trifle wild, there was enough substance to make the atmosphere unhealthy."

In *Motorcycle and Cycle Trader*, David Redgrave echoed Colonel Gray's sentiments by suggesting that the rally should comprise a "hard-core" event embodying the major components of the present rally, with fairly limited entry and fewer field events. He proposed scrapping the Sunday parade in order to devote the whole day to the one-lap regularity test. He also called for the scrapping of the 12-hour event, leaving only the 24-, as with only pairs competing, no rider would have to complete more than five consecutive laps. He suggested that the '24' should have a 'Le Mans-type' area set up at the grandstand containing fairs, stalls, drinks and entertainment for

IOM Scooter Club displays its 1959 rally awards at the Alex Inn. (IOMSC)

the general public, claiming that the entertainment "fell flat." Despite these criticisms, Redgrave concluded that "whatever the form of the Manx Scooter Rally next year, I certainly intend to be on the island for it, and, I hope, for many years to come."

The Isle of Man Scooter Club won more awards than any other club during June's International Scooter Rally, and at a dinner held at the Alex Inn in September, Mr Wilfred Halsall of the Manx Motor Cycle Club proposed a toast to the success of the club, capped by the award of the Lambretta and Wallace Cups, the IOM Championship, and the Assembly Rally first prize to Harold Rowell, who narrowly missed out on the overall championship. Halsall stated that "despite its youth, I must express gratitude to you all for the realistic way in which you have entered this new and important development of two-wheeled transport and, for that matter, two-wheeled sport." Special praise went to J B Bolton, MHK, for his great effort and support.

Club secretary Maureen MacKay was the only female rider in the 24-hour manufacturer team event, in which club team members had all gained at least third class awards. In the 12-hour event, three out of ten first class awards had been won by Alan Henry, Frank Highfield, and Harold Rowell. Mr Rowell also spoke at the event, praising

the help the club – and the scooter tests on the TT course – received from Pat Callin, Edgar Cottier, and Albert Latham. They were the "salt of the earth," he concluded. To round off a successful evening, a Lambretta film of the June 1959 rally was shown, the projectionist being Mr Jack Kermode of Express Radio.[29]

The question later arose whether the Isle of Man Scooter Club should affiliate to the National Scooter Association (NSA), and was discussed in the 1959 Club AGM, when Harold Rowell stressed the need for insurance coverage, and national rules and regulations in the running of competitive events. Affiliation would bring the club within the framework of the ACU, enabling it to secure large concessions in insurance premiums. The case was put forward by a Mr Hills, a guest from the NSA. Caution was urged by Edgar Cottier, vice president and rally organiser, as the club held an international license that could be taken away by a parent body. It was decided to hold a further meeting to discuss this issue, at which Harold Rowell would be deputised as club representative.[30] Although club membership was down slightly, there were more active members than in the previous year.

Chapter 4

1960: ROADS CLOSED

The date of the 1960 rally was announced as June 25; an "outstanding and welcome feature" of which was that certain sections of the Injebreck-Druidale circuit would be closed for the special elimination contest to decide the event's overall winner. The closed section consisted of the Injebreck road in the parishes of Braddan and Michael, from its junction with the roads leading to East and West Baldwin near to the Injebreck reservoir, to its junction with the Beinn-y-Phott Road near Brandywell Cottage. The Druidale road, falling in the parishes of Ballaugh and Michael, was to close from its junction with the Beinn-y-Phott road. Highway and Transport Board permission had already been obtained, and it was hoped that this move would do much to eliminate complaints from several competitors that, on roads open to other traffic, set speeds were "too high and perilous."

Details of the forthcoming rally were issued by rally secretary Pat Callin, and although each event would have its own award, the road events would be grouped to determine major award winners. Events that counted toward the overall trophy were a 'Monte Carlo-type 'rally; a one-lap reliability trial of the TT course, and the 12- and 24-hour tests. Mr Callin claimed that the committee's attention had been consistently drawn to the fact that the 24-hour event was the most coveted award, and that, as further incentive, any driver who obtained a first class award in the 24-hour event would receive a bonus mark to offset penalty marks incurred in other events that counted toward overall rally awards.[31]

Cause for concern about the 1960 event arose when Lambretta announced it would not be supplying official works entries, followed by a similar statement from Douglas, the UK franchise of the Vespa marque, which declared that "No doubt there will be many Vespas in the event, but there is unlikely to be one entered or sponsored by Douglas, or the Vespa Club of Great Britain." Better news came from Bond, which pledged two

factory-supported teams, with works riders competing on the P4 electric self-starting models. In addition, Villiers Engineering and Dunlop promised full support for the rally. It was claimed that if it hadn't been for Villiers encouraging British scooter manufacturers to use their engines to take part, there wouldn't have been a manufacturers' section.[32]

The *Green Final*, published on 5 March, also reported that British teams were giving full support, whilst concessionaires for foreign teams were not, thus putting the future of the rally in jeopardy. Controversy resulted from Peter Agg of Lambretta Concessionaires Ltd announcing that the company would not be entering any works teams, nor providing any facilities for British Lambretta Owners Association members visiting the

The Bond works team of 1960. (IOMSC)

27

island. He pointed out that the previous year's experience had prompted the company to ask for amendments and improvements to the event's organisation, including a better system of regulations, more positive markings, better press facilities, and better hotel accommodation and social facilities for visitors to the island. Agg claimed that Jim Cain of the Tourist Board was unable to provide the firm assurances he required in this respect. His sentiments were echoed by Mr Claude McCormack of (Vespa) Douglas Ltd, who took exception to the fact that the Tourist Board had fixed dates and arrangements without advising manufacturers and concessionaires. Speaking for himself and Peter Agg of Lambretta, he stated that "neither of us takes kindly to virtually being told what we are going to do or when we are going to do it."

An opposing view was printed in the same newspaper by Vespa dealer and rally participant Andre Baldet, who responded by making an urgent appeal for all to support the rally: "I am looking forward to this year's Isle of Man Rally, with or without manufacturer support; with or without the oil companies and the buckshee plug – but with the friendship and the company of other enthusiasts who will enjoy riding for the sake of the sport in an island which has been, for half a century, the Mecca of all two-wheel [bike] owners the world over." In its defence, the Tourist Board announced that, in January, it had organized a 'Personal Service Scooter Holiday Plan' for visitors to the 1960 rally, including full board accommodation (packed meals in lieu when ordered in advance), with garaging and parking when required.

Despite the lack of participation by official Lambretta and Vespa teams, entrants for road-based events totalled 180, which included 103 for the 12-hour reliability rest and 41 for the 24-hour event, with Pat Callin acknowledging the very satisfactory support from individual scooterists. The rules were changed slightly, requiring the first rider in the 24-hour test to stay in the driving seat for 12 hours before handing over to the second rider. Engine classes were arranged from A-D, depending on size, with A class machines covering 21 laps (792.5 miles/1275.41km) at an average 33mph (53.1kph), down to 17 laps (641.75 miles/1032.8km) at 30mph (48.28kph) for Class D. Six manufacturer teams were entered: two from Bond; two from DKR; one from Panther Princess, and one Phoenix team. An American entry was an individual rider, Charles Benson of San Francisco. Thames Valley Vespa Club, winner of last year's team award, also confirmed its participation, and an entry was received from the previous year's Senior Manx Grand Prix winner, Eddie Crooks, riding a 150cc Iso in the 24-hour reliability test.

Entries continued to come in, and by the start of the

rally *Holiday News* reported that scooterists from all over Britain would converge on the island at the conclusion of the 'Monte-Carlo-type' Assembly Rally, with starting points at London, Liverpool, Northampton, Newcastle, and Stirling, each completing a 250 mile (402.34km) route before arriving in Douglas. Competitors now totalled 220, including for road and field events. New awards were to be made, along with cash prizes to the value of £1000, with the Tynwald Trophy going to the outright winner of the entire rally, and Manxland Trophy to the winner in the manufacturer class, the trophies themselves especially constructed from black bog oak and silver.

The scooterists duly arrived on Saturday evening, many of whom had been riding since midnight on Friday. Eddie Crooks was one of the competitors leaving from Newcastle, who reported foggy conditions on his way to Hawick before heading south toward the Lake District. A number of riders complained about the late departure of the afternoon steamer from Liverpool, which meant that registration at the grandstand did not complete until 9pm. The civic reception at the Villa Marina followed this, where the scooterists were welcomed by the Mayor; also present was Bert Kershaw, making his first re-acquaintance with the TT course after an absence of 35 years. He first competed in the TT races in 1921, securing 15th place in the 1923 Junior Race. Another competitor was 18-year-old Mick Bancroft, who hoped to gain experience for his Manx Grand Prix debut in September.

The weather remained fine on Sunday, and large numbers of holidaymakers turned out to cheer on the competitors, as they made their way from Victoria Pier for the grand parade along the promenade. A police car led the way, followed by the RAC patrolette and 180 scooterists. At the grandstand, each rider was required to take part in a simple braking test, accelerating from a line and stopping within a designated distance. A notable failure was Ian Kirkpatrick, secretary of the Scottish Scooter Clubs Association, and member of the Glasgow Vespa Club team, which he blamed on "a build-up of rubber dust in the braking area." After the test, machines were examined for mechanical faults, and crash helmets were examined for signs of deterioration and correct adjustment.[33] At 2.30pm that afternoon, local rider Malcolm Black, on a Dayton machine, was first rider away on the one-lap reliability trial around the TT course, followed at half-minute intervals by the rest of the field.

On Sunday evening, 14 scooters lined up in Noble's Park for the Concours d'Elegance competition. Mrs Didi Baldet followed up on last year's success by winning the 1960 class on her well-prepared Vespa; winner of the pre-1960 class was Mr T G Porter, also on a

Vespa. The judging panel consisted of Mr R A B Cook of *Motorcycling and Scooter Weekly*; Mr Dalton (*Scooter and Three Wheeler*); Mr Vaughan Williams of *Power and Pedal*, and Mr Harold Briercliffe of *Motorcycle and Cycle Trader*, who also distributed the prizes.

On the evening of Monday, June 27, scooterists took to the mountain course for what were described as the most important features of the week – the 12- and 24-hour reliability tests. In the 24-hour event, the first rider now had to ride continuously for 12 hours. Machines were classed from A to D, with riders in the A class category (200cc and over) required to complete 21 laps, totalling over 792 miles (1274.6km), at an average speed of 33mph (53.11kph). The smaller machines in D class (up to 100cc) were required to complete 17 laps (just under 642 miles/1033.2km) at 30mph (48.28kph). Conditions were described as "blustery and variable winds" and, despite riders having to "grope their way through the clammy mist," they were saved the "blinding rain that deluged down in the 1958 reliability tests." Conditions stayed dry until the break of dawn, with the 12-hour riders having completed three-quarters of the required distance. Of the 100-plus riders in the 12-hour event, Vespa and Lambretta machines accounted for 90 per cent of the entry, the remaining scooters being Zundapp, Bella, Dayton, DKR, Maico, Moby, Rumi, Sunbeam, Sun, Phoenix, and Iso.[34]

Rider C Weyman (Maico) was first away from the starting flag of Mr Ron Price from Villiers, the only trade and servicing firm present at the rally. The rest of the field was dispatched at one-minute intervals. Marks were lost for being more than a minute early or late at control points at the rate of one mark per minute. Permanent control points were set up, with temporary ones where snap-checks could be made. Lights came on in the pits as darkness fell, with the petrol staff hard at work throughout the night. An unfortunate incident occurred when Manxman Harold Rowell was splashed in the face with fuel, but with immediate medical treatment, he was able to get away without any penalty marks. A number of minor accidents were reported. The first news of an accident was a report that B A J l'Anson, of the Harrow Lambretta Club, had come off at Signpost Corner. An investigation revealed that sand – which had been spread on melting tar earlier that day – had created a treacherous surface when the tar re-set later that evening. Three-quarters of an hour after the report had been received, another accident occurred when Tony Stroish (DKR), vice-chairman of the National Scooter Association, was involved in an incident with a cattle truck at Brough Jairg Bends. Tony, one of the favourites for the event, sustained bruised ribs when

he diverted into a hedge to avoid the truck, forcing his retirement and putting Auto Scooter Services out of the running for the team award.[35] D A Wilson (Lambretta), a member of 'The Pirates,' suffered from a split fuel tank at Hillberry. J P Francis (Phoenix) was also forced to retire at Hillberry, suffering from engine seizure.

Also in trouble was Andre Baldet on his Vespa sidecar outfit: he had been given a card with the wrong speed schedule, and, having adhered to it, discovered that when he arrived back at the pits he was six minutes late. The points deducted were duly reinstated before he continued on his way. At 11.35pm, Eddie Crooks' Iso had to have a gear change cable replaced, and shortly after midnight, Patricia Aldridge (Lambretta) came in to report that the mist had returned. At the same time, the Catten Brothers, competing in their Dayton sidecar outfit, were reported to have retired at Sulby with a melted piston.

The Bond scooters were the talking point of the night: six of them circulating with "clockwork precision," three of which in the hands of Lancashire policemen. By 2am the weather was "very cold," although officials, helpers and the remaining spectators found respite in the *Motor Cycling* hospitality tent, which served up hot soup and bacon and sausage rolls, along with hot drinks.

By this time, the rigours of the TT course were proving too much for some machines. I Lee (DKR) retired at Creg-ny-Ba with fuse trouble, and M Catten on the Dayton sidecar retired at Sulby with a melted piston, having covered the previous lap with a blowing gasket. A F Price (Lambretta) came off but managed to continue with twisted forks, Alan Henry (Maico) retired without ignition or lights, A W Aldridge (Lambretta) had mechanical failure, and Manxman Tommy Jennings (Lambretta) was forced to retire with carburettor trouble, having previously lost only one mark. Harold Rowell, Dudley Kneen, Sandra Lord, Anne Corlett, Albert Quayle, and Maureen McKay (all on Lambretta machines), and Malcolm Black (Dayton) achieved great success for the Manx contingent, finishing their 12-hour stints without loss of marks shortly before 7am, and thus gaining first class awards. Miss Muriel Gelling and her co-driver completed the 24-hour event without loss of marks.

The field events were held on Wednesday afternoon and evening, controlled by the clerk to the course, and included the slow scooter race, obstacle race, up-and-down the plank race, and the team race, which was run on four separate tracks. Riders from each team stood with their machines at the starting line of each track. On a signal, the rider on track one rode halfway down the track and stopped between two marked lines. With the machine on its centre stand, the plug was removed and replaced,

Main: Sandra Lord puts in an impressive performance on the Druidale circuit. (IOMSC)

Inset: Sandra Lord, riding machine no 7, lines up for the Loving Cup competition. (IOMSC)

and, once 'spanner-tight,' the rider proceeded to the end of the track, parking up in another marked bay. Rider 1 then ran to the second track to hand over the baton to the next rider, who completed an obstacle course before passing the baton to rider three, who also completed the course. Rider four completed the plank race track, during which there was a stop and start test. The rider then parked his machine between marked lines, and ran round to the front of it, holding up his arm to indicate a completed lap.

An astute competitor, Les Moore recalled that, in one particular event, competitors had to grab an apple out of the water tub when the music stopped, signalled by Stan Wardell. Les noticed that Stan gave the signal by lowering his programme behind his back. By running to the barrel as soon as his hand twitched, Les and his team partner, Muriel Gelling, were able to win this event. The remaining races were the wheelbarrow and pram race (in which Les remembers being tipped to the ground), and the zigzag race, with the Scooter Girl and Loving Cup competitions following. The Scooter Girl event was judged on "attractiveness of the driver, the machine, and the driver and the machine combined," and the Loving Cup was awarded to "the most attractive combination of girl, boy and scooter." The scooter had to be driven by the girl – who had to be either a fully licensed or learner driver[36] – into the judging area.

At 9.30am on Thursday, June 30, the 32 machines that had qualified for the Druidale elimination test were released from the impounding marquee, and at 10.05 Harold Rowell was flagged off on his Lambretta, with the remaining riders leaving at one-minute intervals. The course included two sections of the TT course, and two other sections of narrow, twisting back roads which were closed to other traffic.

Pat Aldridge was out of the running, having twisted her handlebars during a practice run, but Venia Bottono and Sandra Lord both rode well for the ladies. Following his performance at Druidale, the title of King of the 1960 International Scooter Rally was awarded to 22-year-old John Thistlethwaite from Bolton, who competed on a

machine he had borrowed only the previous week, in order to take the place of a prospective entrant who was forced to withdraw. Thistlethwaite dropped only 150 marks on the gruelling and very strictly marked Injebreck and Druidale circuit, and was duly presented with the Tynwald Trophy.

The Bond Number 1 team established that the water-splash section could be taken at 50mph, but on Thursday evening – according to *Scooter and Three Wheeler's* August report – the section was considerably deeper than on the previous day. Ken Richardson of the Bond Number 1 team duly crashed, escaping with minor injuries, whilst Vespa rider B A Argent also crashed on the Druidale section, dislocating his shoulder. There were reports of cars on the 'roads closed' section, along with scooterists freely walking about. Under Manx law, this could incur a £20 fine, but luckily there were no serious incidents.

The Douglas Trophy for the manufacturer class individual award was won by ICI assistant technical officer Tom Thorpe. The manufacturer class team award went to the Bond Number 2 team – all traffic police from Preston, led by Sergeant Harry Goldsmith.

Venia Bottono, a 21-year-old shorthand typist from Bromley, was voted Scooter Girl. She also entered the Loving Cup competition, only to find that her pillion passenger hadn't turned up. She turned to a fellow enthusiast, Graham Kneen from Preston, to ask if he would partner her in the competition, to which, *Holiday News* assured its readers, his wife was in full agreement. The pair won the trophy, presented by J B Brooks and Co Ltd. Venia's performance on the Injebreck and Druidale circuit also led to her being crowned Scooter Queen, slightly ahead of Sandra Lord. Both women had gained first-class awards in the Assembly Rally, the one-lap reliability trial, and in the 12-hour regularity test. Miss Lord was a member of the three-strong IOM Scooter Club B Team, which was outright winner of the team award.

Prize presentation took place at the Douglas Holiday Camp on the Friday evening when hundreds of scooterists crowded into the ballroom to hear the Chairman of the Tourist Board, Jim Cain, introduce the Lieutenant Governor and Lady Garvey. Mr Cain claimed it had been a successful rally, and hoped that the scooterists would return the following year in even greater number. Although the rally was hailed a success, it was hoped, said Mr Cain, that abstaining concessionaires would also return for the 1961 event.

Chapter 5

1961: MANX ONE-TWO FOR THE PREMIER AWARDS

Checkpoints for the 1961 Assembly Rally were situated in London, Liverpool, Northampton, Newcastle, Stirling and Bovey Tracy. An innovation for this year was the national hill climb event on June 27, held on the Slough road of the Round Table, with roads closed in addition to the Druidale-Injebreck closure.

On Friday evening, 160 machines embarked on the journey to Liverpool from six starting points, with 149 arriving on Saturday afternoon in brilliant sunshine. The evening was spent at a get-together in the *Motorcycling with Scooter Weekly* marquee behind the grandstand, where competitors were officially greeted by the Mayor of Douglas, Alderman Tom Quirk, JP. Results were announced for the Assembly Rally; Tony Wilson of the Thames Valley Vespa Club pushing Jeff Brown of the Lambretta 'Vagabonds' into 2nd place by less than a second.

continued page 49

Scooters disembark at Victoria Pier, many having taken part in the assembly rally. (IOMSC)

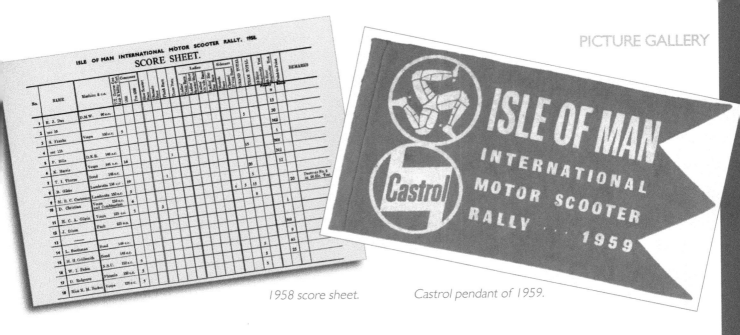

1958 score sheet. *Castrol pendant of 1959.*

Schedules for the 12- and 24-hour regularity tests.

SCHEDULES FOR 12 AND 24 HOUR REGULARITY TESTS

CLASS "A" 12 & 24 HOURS. 33.03 m/h—1 min. 49 (.045) secs. per mile.—68 mins. 34 (.28) secs. per lap.

Appx. Miles		1	2	3	4	5	6	7	8	9	10	11	
		h. m. s.	h. m. s.	h. m. s.	h. m. s.	h. m. s.	h. m. s.	h. m. s.	h. m. s.	h. m. s.	h. m. s.	h. m. s.	
0	Start	0	1-08-34	2-17-08	3-25-42	4-34-17	5-42-51	6-51-25	7-59-59	9-08-34	10-17-08	11-25-42	Start
14½	Kirk Michael (Car Park)	26-15	1-34-49	2-43-23	3-51-57	5-00-32	6-09-06	7-17-40	8-26-14	9-34-49	10-43-23	11-51-57	Kirk Michael (Car Park)
23¾	Ramsey (Square)	43-08	1-51-42	3-00-16	4-08-50	5-17-25	6-25-59	7-34-33	8-43-07	9-51-42	11-00-16	12-08-50	Ramsey (Square)
34½	Creg-ny-Baa (Corner)	1-02-41	2-11-15	3-19-49	4-28-23	5-36-58	6-45-32	7-54-06	9-02-40	10-11-15	11-19-49	12-28-23	Creg-ny-Baa (Corner)
37¾	Pits	1-08-34	2-17-08	3-25-42	4-34-17	5-42-51	6-51-25	7-59-59	9-08-34	10-17-08	11-25-42	12-34-18	Pits

CLASS "A" 24-HOUR		12	13	14	15	16	17	18	19	20	21	
		h. m. s.	h. m. s.	h. m. s.	h. m. s.	h. m. s.	h. m. s.	h. m. s.	h. m. s.	h. m. s.	h. m. s.	
0	Start	12-34-18	1-42-52	2-51-26	4-00-00	5-08-35	6-17-09	7-25-43	8-34-17	9-42-51	10-51-25	Start
14½	Kirk Michael (Car Park)	1-00-33	2-09-07	3-17-41	4-26-15	5-34-50	6-43-24	7-51-58	9-00-32	10-09-06	11-17-40	Kirk Michael (Car Park)
23¾	Ramsey (Square)	1-17-26	2-26-00	3-34-34	4-43-08	5-51-43	7-00-17	8-08-51	9-17-25	10-25-59	11-34-33	Ramsey (Square)
34½	Creg-ny-Baa (Corner)	1-36-59	2-45-33	3-54-07	5-02-41	6-11-16	7-19-50	8-28-24	9-36-58	10-45-32	11-54-06	Creg-ny-Baa (Corner)
37¾	Pits	1-42-52	2-51-26	4-00-00	5-08-35	6-17-09	7-25-43	8-34-17	9-42-51	10-51-25	12-00-00	Pits

9

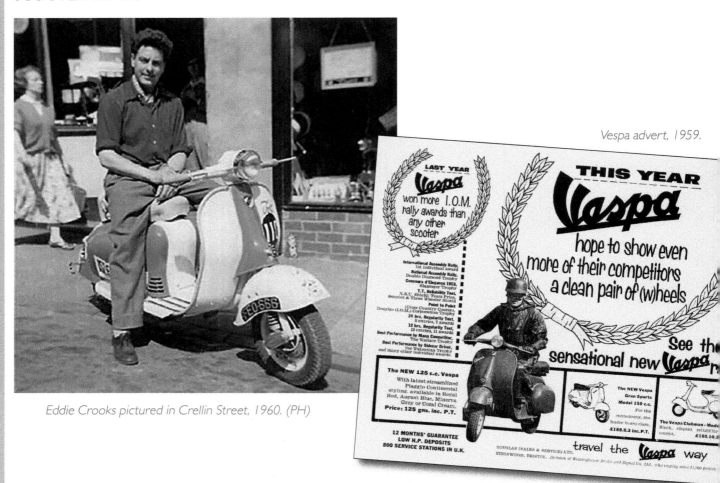

Eddie Crooks pictured in Crellin Street, 1960. (PH)

Vespa advert, 1959.

Castrol pendant of 1960.

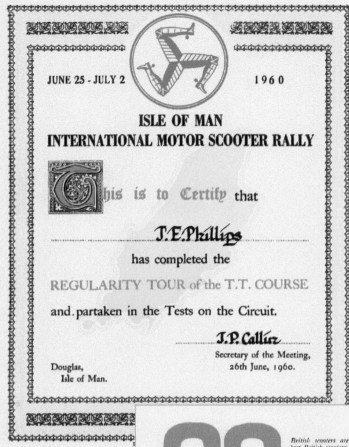

J E Phillips Regularity Tour, 1960.

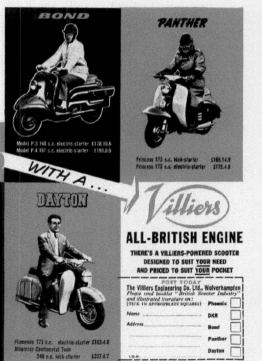

British scooter advert, 1960.

1960 regulation sheet.

Promotional flyer from 1960.

1960 programme.

1961 programme.

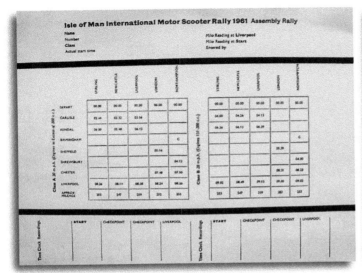

Assembly Rally, 1961.

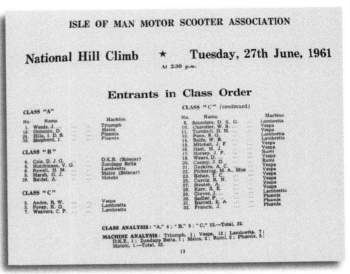

National hill climb, 1961.

LIST OF AWARDS

Basis of Award	Awards	Donor
Premier Award.	Tynwald Trophy and £15.	I.O.M. Scooter Association.
Rally Team Award.	Shield and £15.	"Scooter and Three Wheeler."
Scooter Queen.	Trophy, Rep. and £5.	"Power and Pedal."
Isle of Man Championship.	Trophy, Rep. and £5.	C. Wallace, Esq.
Assembly Rally.	1st and 2nd Class Medallions.	I.O.M. Scooter Association.
Assembly Rally—Individual.	Prize and £3, and 2nd Prize.	Waddingtons Gloves Ltd.
Assembly Rally—Team.	Trophy, Rep. and 3 Medals.	Double Diamond.
24 Hours—Individual.	1st, 2nd and 3rd Class Awards (Mounted Medallions).	I.O.M. Scooter Association.
24 Hours—Team.	6 Medals.	I.O.M. Scooter Association.
12 Hours—Individual.	1st, 2nd and 3rd Class Awards (Mounted Medallions).	I.O.M. Scooter Association.
12 Hours—Team.	3 Medals.	I.O.M. Scooter Association.
Concours pre 1961.	Trophy, Rep., £5, and 2nd Prize.	Slazengers Ltd.
Concours 1961.	Trophy, Rep., £5, and 2nd Prize.	Slazengers Ltd.
Pathfinders.	Group Prizes.	Thanet Travel Goods.
Field Events.	Cups and Cash Prizes.	I.O.M. Scooter Association.
Scooter Girl.	Lycett Rose Bowl and Medallion.	J. B. Brooks & Co., Ltd.
Loving Cup.	Lycett Loving Cup and Medallion.	J. B. Brooks & Co., Ltd.
Best Performance by Villiers. Engined Scooter.	Villiers Award.	Villiers Engineering Co., Ltd.
Best Performance by Competitor from North West London.	Raymond Way Challenge Trophy.	Raymond Way, Esq.
Best Performance by British Scooter.	Harold Day Challenge Trophy.	D.K.R. Scooters Ltd.
Best Sidecar Performance.	Watsonian Challenge Trophy.	Watsonian Sidecars Ltd.
Best Lambretta Driver.	Lambretta Challenge Trophy.	Lambretta Concessionaires Ltd.
Best Maico Driver.	Maico Challenge Trophy.	Maico Scooters.
Best Kent Competitor.	Angus Herbert Challenge Shield.	Angus Motor-Cycles.
Best Vespa Driver.	Vespa Award.	Vespa Club of Great Britain.
Hard Luck Award—12 Hour Event.	Geneva Motors Trophy.	Geneva Motors Ltd.
Hill Climb—Fastest Time of Day.	Cup, £3 (See below).	I.O.M. Scooter Association.
Hill Climb—Class Winners.	1st, £1 and Cup: 2nd, £1; 3rd, 10s.	I.O.M. Scooter Association.

Note: The winner of the Hill Climb Fastest Time of the Day Award is not eligible for his/her appropriate Class Award.

List of awards 1961.

Approx. Miles	CHECKPOINT	LAP 1 h.m.s.	LAP 2 h.m.s.	LAP 3 h.m.s.	LAP 4 h.m.s.	LAP 5 h.m.s.	LAP 6 h.m.s.	LAP 7 h.m.s.	LAP 8 h.m.s.	LAP 9 h.m.s.	LAP 10 h.m.s.	LAP 11 h.m.s.
0.00	START	0.00.00	1.12.00	2.24.00	3.36.00	4.48.00	6.00.00	7.12.00	8.24.00	9.36.00	10.48.00	12.00.00
2.00	2nd Milepost	0.08.33	1.20.33	2.32.33	3.44.33	4.56.33	6.08.33	7.20.33	8.32.33	9.44.33	10.56.33	12.08.33
9.44	½ Way	0.21.47	1.33.47	2.45.47	3.57.47	5.09.47	6.21.47	7.33.47	8.45.47	9.57.47	11.09.47	12.21.47
12.50	Michael (Approach)	0.29.00	1.41.00	2.53.00	4.05.00	5.17.00	6.29.00	7.41.00	8.53.00	10.05.00	11.17.00	12.29.00
16.88	½ Way	0.38.30	1.50.30	3.02.30	4.14.30	5.26.30	6.38.30	7.50.30	9.02.30	10.14.30	11.26.30	12.38.30
25.35	Gooseneck	0.49.47	2.01.47	3.13.47	4.25.47	5.37.47	6.49.47	8.01.47	9.13.47	10.25.47	11.37.47	12.49.47
28.11	½ Way	0.55.15	2.07.15	3.19.15	4.31.15	5.43.15	6.55.15	8.07.15	9.19.15	10.31.15	11.43.15	12.55.15
34.50	Creg	1.06.12	2.18.12	3.30.12	4.42.12	5.54.12	7.06.12	8.18.12	9.30.12	10.42.12	11.54.12	13.06.12
37.77	FINISH	1.12.00	2.24.00	3.36.00	4.48.00	6.00.00	7.12.00	8.24.00	9.36.00	10.48.00	12.00.00	13.12.00

CLASS "B" 31.40 m.p.h.   **"MANX 400"**   TIME PER LAP 72 mins.

IT IS THE DRIVER'S RESPONSIBILITY TO SEE THAT HIS TIME IS ENTERED ON OFFICIAL SHEET BY THE MARSHAL

The Organisers will not accept any responsibility for damage, accident or injury received in any circumstances.

Manx 400 score card from 1962.

1962 programme.

ISLE OF MAN MOTOR SCOOTER RALLY. 1962   JUNE 9th to 16th

SOUVENIR PROGRAMME — ISSUED FREE

THE ENTHUSIASTS "RALLY" TO......

ISLE OF MAN SCOOTER RALLY

1958 Concours d'Elegance—A. Baldet (Vespa G.S.).
Watsonian Trophy for best side-car performance—D. Christian (Vespa 150 with Bambini).
Winner of Scooter-Cross — D. Christian (Vespa G.S.).
Best Manx Competitor—D. Christian (Vespa G.S.).

1959 Concours d'Elegance—E. Baldet (Vespa 152L2).
Members of winning Manufacturers' Team—A. Baldet, D. Christian (Vespa G.S.).

" We ride 'em as well as sell 'em "

MOTO BALDET

for all that is best in scooters and three-wheelers

●

Vespa specialists and distributors of their now famous "Arc-n-ciel" dual tone Vespas (winners of Isle of Man Scooter Rally "Concours d'Elegance" 1958, 1959, 1960).

●

SCOOTERS

D.K.R.	CAPRI
RALEIGH	B.S.A.
VESPA	HEINKEL
ISO	JAMES
DIANA	TRIUMPH

THREE-WHEELER LIGHT CARS

BOND MINICAR	FIAT
TROJAN	RENAULT
ISETTA	N.S.U.
SKODA	MORGAN

●

MOTOR BALDET LIMITED   Telephone : 5751/2
MOTO'S CORNER ———————————— NORTHAMPTON

Island Development Company Ltd., Douglas

Andre Baldet advert from the 1962 programme.

Manx National Heritage
Eiraght Ashoonagh Vannin

Isle of Man Motor Scooter Rally, 1963   June 22nd to 29th

SOUVENIR PROGRAMME — Issued Free by the Isle of Man Tourist Board.

1963 programme.

DOUGLAS
ISLE OF MAN

SUNDAY
23 JUNE 1963

ISLE OF MAN
MOTOR SCOOTER RALLY

This is to Certify that

Mrs. P.E. Crooks

has completed the
SUNDAY SPIN
with the loss of **2** marks.

J. P. CALLIN
Secretary of the Meeting

*Pauline Crooks,
Sunday Spin, 1963.*

*Sandra Lord, Sunday
Spin, 1963.*

DOUGLAS
ISLE OF MAN

SUNDAY
23 JUNE 1963

ISLE OF MAN
MOTOR SCOOTER RALLY

This is to Certify that

Miss S. Lord

has completed the
SUNDAY SPIN
with the loss of **1** marks.

J. P. CALLIN
Secretary of the Meeting

Manxman Terry Moore competes in the scrambling event at Ballacallin. (TM)

1964 programme.

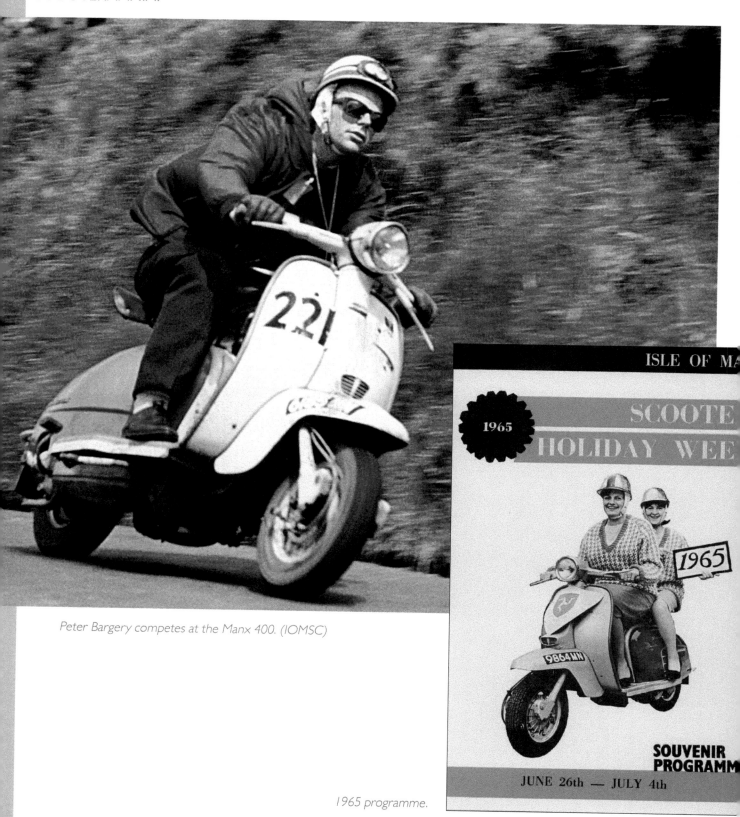

Peter Bargery competes at the Manx 400. (IOMSC)

ISLE OF MA

1965

SCOOTE

HOLIDAY WEE

1965

SOUVENIR
PROGRAMM

JUNE 26th — JULY 4th

1965 programme.

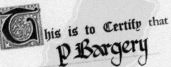

Peter Bargery, Manx 400, 1965.

1966 programme.

1967 programme.

JUNE 24
JULY 1
1967

ISLE
OF
MAN

SCOOT

APH BY COURTESY OF W. H. HEAPS

R HOLIDAY WEEK!

Terry Moore competing at the Ramsey sprint. (TM)

The inaugural night trial event. (IOMSC)

TT course.

Terry Moore negotiates the water-splash at Druidale. (TM)

Lambretta

announce that the overall rally champion of the 1967 Isle of Man Scooter Rally, if riding a Lambretta, will win a holiday for two in Italy with his Lambretta or a cash prize of £100.

Additional awards for Lambretta riders include £15.15.0 vouchers donated by Hepworths hand cut tailoring to best Lambretta on Druidale and in the gymkhana. Special other Hepworth discount vouchers for outstanding performers.

THE BEST OF BRITISH LAMBRETTA LUCK.

Lambretta prize award, 1967.

The Thames Valley A Team was awarded the team prize.

On Sunday, June 25, riders reported to the parade marshal at Victoria Pier at 10am, then proceeded along a selected route to the TT grandstand: any rider failing to take part incurred 20 penalty points in the overall competition for premier awards, unless exemption was granted by the clerk to the course. Following the parade, the Concours d'Elegance took place at Noble's Park. In the pre-1961 class, there were 16 entries, with just half a mark separating the winner, P Gannon (Lambretta and sidecar), and R H Imray, also on a Lambretta. The winning red and black Lambretta and sidecar was "equipped with every luxury, including radio, reading lamp, rev counter and fire extinguisher."[37] In the '61 class (six entries), first place went to M B Ninnim (Vespa), who had been persuaded to enter his machine at the last minute, and second place was awarded to J Brown (Lambretta). In the afternoon, scrutineering took place, followed by acceleration and braking tests, the average being around 4.5 seconds from start to finish..

The one-lap reliability event was omitted from the programme in order to facilitate the hill climb event later in the week. The 12- and 24-hour events began on Sunday at 6pm, ensuring that all riders had time to become acclimatised with the course before the weather deteriorated. It was reported that riders in the reliability trial were hampered by wind and rain throughout the night, and that 115 riders had left the grandstand on Sunday evening, led by last year's overall winner, John Thistlethwaite. The riders were flagged away by the Mayor, Alderman Tom Quirk, with the downpour becoming progressively worse, as did the mist. *Motorcycling with Scooter Weekly* reported on June 29 that there were "skids, mechanical breakdowns and retirements due to the sheer inability to see through dimmed goggles."

By 9am on Monday morning, 59 entrants remained in the competition. 19 riders completed the distance without losing any marks; 21 lost ten marks (2nd class award), and 19 lost 30 marks (3rd class award). Manx girl Maureen MacKay escaped serious injury when the steering on her Lambretta developed trouble descending the mountain in darkness. Approaching Brandish Corner the machine swerved toward the hedge, and its rider managed to leap clear, escaping with shock and bruising only. Keith Brown, a 28-year-old clerk from London, crashed in the mist at Windy Corner and required hospital treatment for a fractured leg. Three other riders retired after falling off, but were unhurt.

Interviewed in 2012, Manxman Les Moore recalled the 1961, event, revealing that whilst travelling through the mountain mist at 50mph (80kph), he was passed by John Thistlethwaite on his Maicoletta, showing only sidelights and barely visible. Les caught up with him at Creg-ny-Baa checkpoint, where John explained that, as he knew the mountain so well, he was preserving the power of his rapidly-draining battery ...

The *Scooter and Three Wheeler* shield for the team award was won by the Thames Valley 'A' team, consisting of A J Wilson, T C Behan, and R E Gregg, who had already won the team award for the Assembly Rally, with the individual award going to Anthony Wilson. Seven minutes robbed 20-year-old Paul Sadler of a third class award – the Harold Day Trophy for best British scooter, and the Villiers award – as a result of his Phoenix scooter experiencing sprocket trouble. The damaged component was rushed to Douglas for emergency welding, but, with three laps still to complete, he could not quite make up the time. The Manx pairings of Harold Rowell and Miss L M Mangan, and R G Pen and Miss J Kneen – both sets of riders on Lambretta machines – were presented with first

Riders gather round Bill Andre's Vespa GS. (MNH)

class awards without loss of marks. Mr Rowell also won the class B section on the hill climb event, with the Class A event going to J Woods on a Triumph.

The road was closed for the new hill climb event on Tuesday afternoon, which comprised a mile-long stretch of the Slough road in Rushen, taking in left- and right-hand bends, and a maximum gradient of 1 in 8. Riders were helped up the course by a strong wind, with the best time of two runs recorded in each case from the 16 riders taking part. D Ormston put in the fastest time of the day on his Maico machine. Harold Rowell (Lambretta) suffered a puncture on his first attempt, but achieved the best time in Class B on his second go. The event was held under a National Scooter Association permit, but did not count toward overall rally positions.[38]

Fourteen riders without loss of marks in the 12-hour regularity test set off on the rally decider, taking them from the grandstand to Injebreck, and over the fast-timed

Premier Award winner Dennis Craine is presented with the Tynwald Trophy. (IOMSC)

section onto the Brandywell, Ballaugh, and tough Druidale section where many riders lost points. Originally, 32 riders should have started the final trial, but a complaint was lodged by one rider who felt that only first class award winners should compete. The complaint was heard by the stewards late on Wednesday, the outcome being that only first class award winners from the 12-hour rally would go forward.

The bad weather abated later in the week, and blue skies were reported for the Injebreck/Druidale event, completed with only one minor casualty (A J Wilson (Vespa) came off at Brandywell Corner), and retirement of the sidecar team of G J Marsh and A T Hicks (Maico) due to mechanical trouble.

When the results came in it was confirmed that the Premier Award had been won by Manxman Dennis Craine (Lambretta), a scooter dealer from Douglas, who competed on a machine from his hire fleet. 26-year-old Dennis from Onchan had been riding motorcycles from the age of 16, and in the previous two years had competed in several major scrambles in the UK. His orange-coloured, 150cc Lambretta had been taken off Hire and Drive service the previous week, and given an overhaul in time for Dennis to take it to Liverpool, and then Carlisle for the Assembly Rally. The Scooter Queen award went to 17-year-old Sylvia Kelly from Douglas, who had been riding for less than a year. The Scooter Girl award was claimed by Miss M G S Hutchinson, and the Loving Cup, sponsored by J B Brooks and Co Ltd (Saddles and Accessories) was awarded to R M Rawlings and Pauline Stubbs by the sponsor's sales manager, K M Rawlings.

Riders of combo 96 – G J Marsh and A T Hicks – compete in the hill climb event. (MNH)

Inset: Rider no 7, M Claxton, also on the hill climb. (MNH)

R M Rawlings and Pauline Stubbs, winners of the Loving Cup competition. (MNH)

Scooter girl of 1961, Miss M G S Hutchinson, shows off her trophy. (MNH)

Chapter 6

1962: THE MANX 400 AND SCOOT TO SCOTLAND

Riders disembark in 1962: Manx rider Kenny Radcliffe is on scooter no 55. (MNH)

Changes for the 1962 event were not only intended to facilitate an enjoyable week for all scooterists, but, in order to provide a spectacle, the three tough road events would be completed by hardier competitors. The rally – due to "circumstances beyond the control of the organizing committee" – was set for the week following the TT races, which clashed some with 'Scoot to Scotland,' another major event on the scootering calendar. This was an

Assembly Rally, sponsored by Esso, and organised by the Motor Cycling Club, now in its sixth year, with starting points throughout the UK. Staging the event at this time would give TT spectators the option of remaining on the island to see the rally, and those scooterists who wished to take part in the Scottish event could still arrive on the island in time to compete for the top prizes.

More checkpoints were planned for the 'Manx 400'

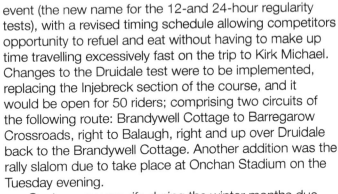

N T A Atterbom sets off after a pit-stop. (IOMSC)

Manx rider Norman Moore leaving the grandstand on the Manx 400. (NM)

event (the new name for the 12-and 24-hour regularity tests), with a revised timing schedule allowing competitors opportunity to refuel and eat without having to make up time travelling excessively fast on the trip to Kirk Michael. Changes to the Druidale test were to be implemented, replacing the Injebreck section of the course, and it would be open for 50 riders; comprising two circuits of the following route: Brandywell Cottage to Barregarow Crossroads, right to Balaugh, right and up over Druidale back to the Brandywell Cottage. Another addition was the rally slalom due to take place at Onchan Stadium on the Tuesday evening.

Controversy was rife during the winter months due to a serious delay in distributing the regulations and entry forms for the 1962 event, still waiting approval from the National Scooter Association in February, which demanded that competition licences must be held by riders in the Manx 400. This was bitterly opposed by the organisers, who were to send two representatives to London on the 17th of that month to plead their case with the NSA, believing that this ruling would be detrimental to the rally in particular, and scootering in general. In a letter to the press, club secretary Pat Callin stated that the delay was deeply regretted and not wanted by the club.[39]

Despite this delay, however, final entries for the event

reached 175 – slightly more than in the previous year. Overseas riders included R Pochkanawala from India, and N T A Atterbom from Sweden.

The event kicked off on Saturday, June 9 with the Assembly Rally, and starting points this year were from Northampton, Liverpool, Stirling, Newcastle, Chudleigh, London, and Birmingham. It was arranged to make facilities on the ferry available from 6.30am in order to supply hungry scooterists with hot meals. In the evening, riders headed for the official reception and dance. Late arrivals travelling from the 'Scoot to Scotland' event sailed from Ardrossan on Sunday afternoon. On 11 June the *Daily Mail* ran the header 'The Invaders Go by Scooter,' and reported that, on Sunday, more than 200 machines, travelling four abreast, paraded along the promenade, cheered on by hundreds of holidaymakers, describing the event as "their week of glory, taking over from where their TT Big Brothers left off." In the afternoon, judging took place for the Concours d'Elegance, followed by the preliminary round of the Scooter Girl competition on Douglas promenade.

It was lamentable that the scooter rally did not enjoy the same good weather as the TT races, and the reliability test over the mountain was particularly bad for the second year running, making everything difficult for organisers and competitors alike. The Manx 400 lapped the TT circuit at set distances of 340 miles (547km) and 415 miles (668km), depending on class (determined by engine size). Scrutineering took place on Monday morning, and riders were flagged away in the evening at 9pm, with adverse weather conditions of mist and heavy rain prevailing, and travelling marshals reporting abandoned machines all around the course (first man out was Bill Andre and his Vespa sidecar combination).

Despite atrocious conditions, a large crowd assembled at the grandstand. Riders returning to the pits, having completed the first lap, reported patchy mist from the Verandah on the mountain road, down toward Douglas, but with eight controls operating, split-second timing was even more important to avoid losing marks. The poor road conditions were evidenced by the 71 retirements which ensued, one of whom exclaimed "I do not want to die yet!"[40] It was, therefore, remarkable that 41 riders completed the course.

The all-night marquee did a sterling job by providing food, drink and music to cheer riders on their fuel stops. A reporter for the June issue of *Scooter World* magazine observed that helpers at the refuelling depot were totally overwhelmed at one point as riders came in to refuel, with special praise going to Muriel Gelling and Kenny Radcliffe who, having retired from the rally, pitched in at the refuelling area to help those still competing.

Two riders, Ken Clifford and George Cooper, were dismounted from their Vespas, and were taken to Nobel's hospital for minor treatment. Manxman Terry Moore, participating in his first event of this type, was forced into retirement with a broken shaft. The travelling marshals said at 5am that there were several machines lying around the course without their riders. Andre Baldet dropped his machine at Shepherd's Hut, but managed to restart, and checked in at Creg-ny-Baa without penalty. However, interviewed in 2012, Manx competitor Malcolm Black revealed that Andre was ahead of him in the starting order, yet Malcolm passed him before checking in at Kate's Cottage. Despite Andre's penalty-free check-in, Malcolm was informed that he was a minute late and would lose one point. Despite his protest, the decision was upheld, resulting in a silver award instead of the gold.

The *Daily Mail* reported that a lively atmosphere, along the lines of a 'Le Mans' night, prevailed at the grandstand, with music blaring from the marquee. Jim Cain, chairman of the rally committee, remained there throughout, along with stewards R Penn, Wilf Halsall, and Henry Kelly. Speaking to a *Daily Mail* reporter, Mr Cain said "you must really hand it to these boys and girls. They showed marvellous pluck and endurance, and if it were possible,

Robin Thomas competes with his Maicoletta in the slalom – highlight of the field events. (IOMSC)

I would like to see them all getting a prize."[41] *Scooter and Three Wheeler* magazine reported that, with the exception of the Surbiton Diana Club, the Isle of Man Scooter Club (which entered five teams), South London Scooter Club, and the Glasgow Vespa Club, all big name clubs were absent, yet there was still stiff competition, with the real heroine of the competition being Anne Corlett, who battled her way through twelve "miserable yet exhilarating hours" to become Scooter Queen.[42] However, this result prompted a call from the editor of *Scooter World Magazine* for a "tightening of the rules," as Anne had not run in the Druidale circuit: her first class award in the 400 ensured that nobody competing at Druidale could overturn her lead.

At the end of the Manx 400 event, five riders were level pegging, including Andre Baldet (Vespa), who was the 1960 sidecar champion. First class awards were also awarded to John Thistlethwaite, Bill Andre, John Alexander, I Kirkpatrick, and Miss Anne Corlett. MGP rider Alan Killip, Neil Kelly, and scrambler Ralph Lowey not only won the Manx 400 team prize but also the rally team award on their Raleigh Roma machines. Those competitors who were not sleeping off their exertions from the Manx 400 took part in the field events on Tuesday, with the main feature being the slalom behind the grandstand.

Rider 113, Keith Turns, competes in the plank race. (MNH)

Competitors line up at Druidale to decide the first Premier Award. (IOMSC)

Rider 168, Tony Dunseath, attempts the slow race. (MNH)

Premier Award winner John Alexander receives the Tynwald Trophy. (MNH)

The best weather of the week was saved for the round island navigational trial, starting from Peel on Wednesday. An innovation announced to the press by clerk to the course Stan Wardell, this event was becoming increasingly popular in England, and was run by Clive Weavers, Chief Steward of the London and Home Counties area of the National Scooter Association, who claimed to have plotted the course for the trial at his home in London: "When I took part in the Manx Scooter Rally in 1958," said Clive, "I realized that this small island was more than just a dot on the map. I have visited the island every year since. The riders will enjoy the great contrasts of the countryside in the north and south of the island."[43] Forty-four riders took part, in the saddle for 7 hours, and taking an all-island, 100-mile tour from Peel Promenade, with a route book and map references. Competitors were required to pinpoint such things as a manhole cover somewhere on the island by means of a six-figure map reference.

The Men's Rally Champion was to be decided on the Druidale circuit, the event contested by 35 riders, including the six first class award winners from the Manx 400. Setting off at ten second intervals from Brandywell Cottage, the route took them down to Barregarow, along the TT course to Ballaugh, and back to Brandywell via the Druidale road – each rider completing two laps. The best vantage point was described as the water-splash, where a stream crossed the road at the bottom of a 50mph (80kph) dip.

Whilst leading the field on the second lap, rider Thistlethwaite, Scooter King of 1960, came to grief in a spectacular crash on his Maico machine, losing control coming out of the dip and hitting the bank. He was flung across the road, luckily, sustaining only cuts and bruises, whilst his machine plunged down the ten metre drop at the side of the road. Andre Baldet commented that "conditions were bad, but it wasn't too difficult. It helped a lot if you knew the course." He concluded that this was the event he had enjoyed the most in this year's competition.[44] Only four riders failed to finish.

Previously only open to the best riders in the 12-hour event, this year, the men's rally was open to everyone. The Scooter King title – now known as the Premier Award – was decided on the Druidale circuit, and won by John Alexander from Glasgow on his Vespa. Andre Baldet came in second, making it a successful year for him, as he won the slalom event at Onchan Stadium; came first in the Assembly Rally, and also won the Concours d'Elegance (pre-1962 model). Following the competition at Druidale, scooterists were entertained at a Welcome Dance at the Alex Inn, organised by the Isle of Man Scooter Club.

Debate regarding the date of the following year's rally continued, but was ultimately to be decided by the competitors. Andre Baldet told the *Daily Mail*: "You can hold the IOM rally any time you like. There is nothing like it anywhere." Fellow dealer, Londoner Bill Andre, added: "I attend a lot of rallies and the Manx is always my first and biggest. It launches the scooter season and everything else just follows. It is not affected by clashing with other events. If it was put back to September, it would be coming at the end of the season, and after dozens of

Andre Baldet, winner of the pre-1962 Concours d'Elegance trophy. (IOMSC)

Shirley Rhodes, Scooter Girl of 1962. (IOMSC)

Band Leader Ken Mackintosh judging the winning machine in the 1962 Concours d'Elegance. (MNH)

Winner of the 1962 Concours d'Elegance trophy, Miss Rhyder. (MNH)

Alan 'Kipper' Killip accepts the team prize for the 'Raleigh Romas.' (MNH)

their own club events, scooterists would be tired of competitions. I have talked to a lot of scooterists; they want the Isle of Man to start the summer, not finish it." Dr W E Pyecraft, timekeeper and resident of Douglas, was one of those in favour of the change, due to the number of events already held in June, claiming that "they all come at once. It would be a relief to split them up a bit."[45]

The Scooter Girl award was presented to 26-year-old Shirley Rhodes from Manchester, who was chosen from six finalists in the Royal Hall, Villa Marina on the Thursday evening. She was a member of East Manchester Vespa Club, and had been a finalist in the Loving Cup competition in 1959. This year's Loving Cup went to Cheltenham couple Peter Gregory and his wife, Frances. Scooter Queen Anne Corlett was also the winner of the IOM Championship Award.

The 1962 rally attracted many newcomers to the event, including several of a young age. It was claimed

Peter and Frances Gregory celebrate winning the Loving Cup. (MNH)

Anne Corlett: Scooter Queen of 1962, is presented with her tropy. (IOMSC)

that if the rally hadn't clashed with the event in Scotland, entries would have been even higher, and the suggestion was made that the IOM rally should be the finale of a season of events in September, with fixtures taking place at major UK rallies throughout the summer. It was again suggested that the 1963 scooter rally should follow the MGP in September, in order to avoid clashing with other

scooter events in the UK, and reaction from competitors was favourable. Liverpudlian entrants were quizzed on the matter, and they stated they would be back, regardless of timing, claiming that having been to the IOM rally was "something to talk about"! A number of those asked favoured a September date in the hope of better weather.[46]

Chapter 7

1963: STORM WARNING

Of 1963's 152 entries, half were newcomers, and included competitors from India and Australia. Scooters were scheduled to arrive on the vessel *Manx Maid*, which had a dance band on board to provide entertainment. Following the usual parade and judging of the Concours d'Elegance and Loving Cup competitions, a 'Sunday spin' event was arranged for the afternoon, and another innovation was a music and dance session to be staged in a marquee behind the grandstand from eight o'clock on Monday evening until one o'clock on Tuesday morning. On the Tuesday evening, a social run and gathering for a beach barbecue was planned at Glen Wyllin. Field events were set for Onchan Stadium on Wednesday, with the Loving Cup and Scooter Girl awards taking place on Thursday.

It was claimed that the weather for the 400 was even worse than the previous year, with a mixture of rain, mist and slippery roads. It began raining steadily as a hundred competitors lined up behind the starting ramp at the TT grandstand. Clerk to the course Stan Wardell delivered a formidable weather forecast of strong winds and fog from Guthrie's Memorial to Keppel Gate, with visibility down to 50 metres or less.

Vic Zealey was first away in his Lambretta sidecar outfit, with dance band leader Ivy Benson – well known for her regular appearances at the Villa Marina – wielding the starter's flag. Unfortunately, Zealey was forced to retire in the final stages of the competition when his passenger became ill. Seventh rider on the starting ramp was Eddie Crooks on a Jawa machine, bought to the island for testing. His wife, Pauline, also competed in the 400, her passenger being Brendan Hill from Barrow. First female away was this year's youngest rider, Christine Harris from Devon, also a finalist in the Scooter Girl competition. Christine had hoped to pass her driving test before coming to the island, but the long waiting list in her home town of Bovey Tracey prevented her from being able to leave behind her L plates, and thus barred her

Ivy Benson flags off the Manx 400. (IOMSC)

from entering the 400. However, on reaching the island, her father contacted a driving test official in the Highways Department, and arrangement was made for Christine to fill a vacancy that arose in the day's test programme. She duly passed, and qualified for entry in the big event.[47]

First casualty of the evening was A Roberts (Lambretta), fortunately unhurt when he skidded at Union Mills and hit a wall. A Quayle, also riding a Lambretta, became unseated at Governor's Bridge, which also claimed W Anderson (Vespa). There were several retirements, including P L Newbutt when his Lambretta's engine seized at Ramsey. Glass was also reported on the

Pauline Crooks with Eddie and son, Martin.

Ralph Lowey, Neil Kelly, and Alan Killip pictured with their Raleigh Roma machines. (IOMSC)

Clerk to the course Stan Wardell is presented with an award from Jim Cain, prior to the start of the Manx 400, for his commitment to the rally since its inception. Club secretary Pat Callin is pictured to the left. (MNH)

road at Kirk Michael, and speculation about how it got there was answered when it was discovered that two cars had been involved in a minor accident. 1960 champion John Thistlethwaite was again beset by bad luck, following on from his crash on the Druidale circuit the year before. This year, he had to retire from the 400 when his Heinkel developed generator trouble.

Manx riders Harold Rowell, Ralph Lowey, Alan Killip and Neil Kelly got through the Manx 400 without loss of marks. The team award went to the Manx AEC team, consisting of Malcolm Black, Harold Rowell, and Peter Lees (the team's name was created from the initials of the previous year's Scooter Queen, Anne Elizabeth Corlett, who should have been competing but was ill in hospital). A record number of 19 riders achieved first class awards, despite the horrendous weather conditions, twelve of whom were Manx entrants.

The bad weather continued, and, for the first time in the history of the Isle of Man Scooter Rally, there was no Scooter King, as blanket fog caused the Druidale test – decider of this competition – to be cancelled. The 59 riders arrived at Brandywell to be confronted by thick mist and drizzle. Clerk to the course Stanley Wardell decided that it was too dangerous to start. Hourly weather reports were taken, and revised start times cancelled with each one. The deadline for starting was 4pm, but at 3pm it became apparent that there would be no let-up in the atrocious conditions. Secretary Pat Callin declared that "Both competitors and officials have agreed that the right decision was taken. The riders accepted it, and the officials felt that it was better to cancel completely rather than risk lives. In such weather conditions that would have been the case if the event had gone ahead." Postponing

Malcolm Black receives the team prize for the AEC team. (MB)

the event to the following Friday was not possible, as there was insufficient time to apply for a new road closure notice for the Druidale section of the course. Cancellation of Druidale meant that local girl Sandra Lord (Heinkel) was crowned Scooter Queen for her performance in the Manx 400.

The *Daily Express* reported that out of the scores of pretty girls visiting the Isle of Man for this year's rally, only seven entered the Scooter Girl competition, and six entered the Loving Cup. One of the officials, speaking to the *Express*, stated that "It was the same last year. The girls just won't enter. We can only assume that they are too shy." Entrant Sylvia Kelly from Douglas echoed these sentiments, along with her friend, Sandra Lord, claiming she was too shy to enter the competition.[48] The winner of Scooter Girl 1963 was Mrs Pauline Crooks, wife of Manx 400 rider Eddie. Pauline declared herself "over the moon" with the win, though confessed that she, too, had been reluctant to take part, only to discover that she had been entered by her husband. Interviewed in 2012, Pauline remembers riding on the TT course in very poor weather conditions, with only a flimsy raincoat by way of protection. She did, however, get her father to drive just in front of her, in an attempt to minimize the effects of wind and rain.

The Loving Cup was awarded to computer operator

Sandra Lord, Scooter Queen, 1963, competing in the Manx 400. (IOMSC)

Sandra Blake and her boyfriend, Harvey Watt, both from Glasgow. Winner of the Concours d'Elegance was Phillip Lewis, and winner of the pre-1963 class was Reg Imray from Southend, with his 1957 Lambretta. This vehicle was claimed to have £300 worth of extras, including three headlights, fully chrome-plated engine, special exhaust, compass, clock, temperature gauge, and brake efficiency indicator. It was said that the "glittering chrome-work and sparkling finish" completely stole the show. It was also reported in the *Daily Express* that it had been a bad week for fellow scooterist and motor-racing ace Stirling Moss, who failed his scooter test!

Scooter Girl Pauline Crooks relaxes in front of the crowd. (PH)

Pauline Crooks (far left), Scooter Girl and winner of the Lycett Rose Bowl, pictured next to runner-up Christine Harris, and third-placed Sylvia Kelly. (PH)

Pauline Crooks and Brendan Hill, competitors in the Manx 400, pictured here in the Loving Cup competition at the Villa Marina. (PH)

Left: Loving Cup winners Sandra Blake and Harvey Watt. (MNH)

The big story which broke following the rally was that a 27-year-old Polish competitor, Elizabeth Smolen, had made a brave escape to the West prior to competing in the rally. In 1958, whilst studying at Krakow University, she was selected for the Polish International Motorcycling Team. En route to a competition in Belgium, Elizabeth made a break for freedom from the hotel the team was staying at in Frankfurt at 5am, dressed only in her night clothes. She befriended a German couple who looked after her until she found employment in Hamburg. She also applied for a visa from the British Embassy, and eight months later, arrived on the Wirral to join her father, the proprietor of a motorcycle business. In November 1962, the entire family was re-united when the Polish authorities granted permission for her mother to leave the country.[49]

Chapter 8

1964: FROM BEHIND THE IRON CURTAIN

The Manx sporting publication *Green Final* printed excerpts from the January issue of the Czechoslovak *Motor Review*, detailing the exploits of two "outstanding" motorcyclists, Eddie Crooks and Roger Kelly, in the 1963 Manx 400. The magazine's UK correspondent, J Alexander, told how Eddie and Roger pitted their Jawa 50cc scooters against machines double their class size. For their epic rides, each man received a pendant and medallion from Jawa. The article, featuring illustrations of Eddie and his wife – and Scooter Girl winner – Pauline, was published in several languages, and circulated throughout Europe, the US and Canada, Australia, India, and Japan[50], giving the event the worldwide publicity its organisers sought.

With the closing date still several weeks away, over a hundred entries had been received for the 1964 event, this year to be held between June 20 and 27. It was also announced that a team from Czechoslovakia would be competing on new, 50cc Jawas and 100cc Manets: believed to be their first appearance in Britain. The Assembly Rally mileage was to be calculated by multiplying the number of scooterists in the group by the distance (RAC mileage) from their town of departure to Liverpool. This meant that the more entrants there were, the higher the mileage would be, and the more points to be scored.

The 400 event was to be given a new look, and held on 21 June: scooterists would leave in pairs, with a compulsory 30-minute meal stop after six hours. The scope of the field events was to be extended, with an event in the Bowl in Douglas on the Monday afternoon.

By mid-June, the number of entrants had risen to 185: 30 up on last year's total, and consisted of 100 new entrants, including David Lloyd from the USA. Thirty female riders were to take part, including the 'Gay Nineties' team, riding the new Vespa 90cc. 90 entries for the Manx 400 were received, and 60 for the Druidale trial.

The first social event of the rally was an informal get-together at the Douglas Head Hotel on Saturday evening, with scrutineering for the Manx 400 taking place at 7.30am on Sunday morning. Field events and the Concours d'Elegance were moved from Noble's Park to the King George V Park, followed by the civic reception and dance at the Villa Marina. The pre-1964 class in the Concours d'Elegance was won by T Westfield's Lambretta LD, with Irishman R O Turly victorious in the 1964 class with his Heinkel.

The Manx 400 started off from its new setting on the promenade, opposite the war memorial. For the first time, the event began in the morning, and riders were at liberty to fill up at any petrol station on the course. A refreshment station was set up at Glen Helen, where hungry riders could get a hot meal during their compulsory stop. The Manx team of Neil Kelly, Ralph Lowey, and Allan Killip competed on their Raleigh Roma machines, and the Czechoslovakian riders were named as Ondrej Dorinec, Pavel Cernasky, Rudolf Huncik, and Stefan Oravi, A Bahensky, Hans Holzer and M Joseph, with local riders Brenda Cain (Jawa) and R A Jackson (Manet) joining them to form two teams.

Rally veteran Vic Zealey was again first man away, flagged off by Ivy Benson at 9am, and followed at one-minute intervals by his fellow competitors, with Vespas outnumbering Lambrettas by thirty eight to thirty. First man out of the competition was L H Moore, who dropped his NSU Prima machine at Ballacraine. Two more early retirements were Ralph Lowey and Allan Killip of the Raleigh Roma team, winners of last year's team prize. Miss N Anstead was also involved in an incident at Ballacraine, but fortunately was able to continue. Polish-born Elizabeth Smolen had completed three faultless laps when her Vespa GS seized at the eleventh hour, yet was said to be hoping to have the engine fixed before Tuesday's scrambling event. Czech competitor

Eddie Corkhill prepares to ride away at the start of the Manx 400.

M Joseph completed the event without loss of marks, and revealed that his 98cc Manet scooter had clocked up its 59,000th kilometre on the 10th lap, and that his fellow team member, Hans Holzer, had appealed against a time penalty as he was misdirected by a policeman at Ballacraine. A new record number of 53 riders won first class awards, including two of the Vespa 90 girls, and Manx woman Muriel Brooks.

The treasure hunt was held on Tuesday morning, with 60 competitors taking part. The event was won by R T Young of Rutherglen, and Ann Wallace, from Harlton, a member of the Vespa 90 team. The evening

was dedicated to scrambling at Ballacallin, with practice commencing at 6pm. Clerk to the course for this event was Malcolm Black, and racing got under way at 7pm with the all-comers category, consisting mainly of standard machines. Fourteen machines competed in the nine-lap races, with Luke Kitto of Exeter winning the handicap event. Czech rider Rudolf Huncik won the under 150cc event, and Elizabeth Smolen, following emergency repairs on her engine, came second in the handicap and over 150cc events.

Racing was followed by a party at the Glen Helen, and more field events were held at Onchan on Wednesday, including the slalom and the grass races. Thursday played host to what were described as informal 'disorganised games,' and a fancy dress event at the Bowl, to be held before the Loving Cup and Scooter Girl competitions in the afternoon. As the Scooter Girl competitors assembled their machines, ready to ride up the ramp and onto the stage of the Villa Pavilion, Anne Wallace discovered that one of the entrants from the South Devon Vespa Club, of which she was a member, had not shown up. Previously too shy to enter, despite winning a gold medal in the Manx 400, Anne was persuaded to fill the missing place, and within fifteen minutes, was standing in the gardens in "glorious sunshine" in front of hundreds of holidaymakers as she was presented with the winner's Lycett Silver Rose Bowl. The Loving Cup competition was won by 21-year-old Tom Westfield and his fiancée, 19-year-old Pat Norman, both from Hemel Hempstead.

The Druidale event took place on Friday in perfect conditions, with Roger Crook of Nottingham duly declared Rally Champion, and winner of the Premier Award. Roger, and his team-mates, John and Norman Ronald, were all members of Nottingham Lambretta Club, known as The Bowmen. They scored three gold medals in the Manx 400, and also collected the *Scooter and Three Wheeler* Team Award, the Druidale Award, the Best Newcomer Award, and the Lambretta Challenge Trophy. The title of Scooter Queen was bestowed on Miss N W Anstead.

At the prize giving ceremony held at Douglas Head, special tributes were paid to the Czechoslovakian team and its manager, Mr B B Lindhart, who reported that they had enjoyed their stay, and praised the hospitality received. On Tuesday evening, they had been guests of the Mayor, to whom Mr Lindhart pledged to bring more riders to the event, and to provide their Manx team-mates, Brenda Cain and Rex Jackson, with machinery for next year's rally.[51]

It was also later announced at the ceremony that Vespa and Lambretta would be sponsoring next year's event with assistance from the Tourist Board. In a joint speech made by Bob Wilkinson, secretary of the British Lambretta Owner's Association, and his counterpart from Vespa, Dave Pullom, scooterists were advised that their respective organisations had buried the hatchet, and hoped to make next year's event cheaper to enter. Talks were soon under way between Bob Wilkinson, Dave Pullom, and the Isle of Man Scooter Rally Association with a view to expanding the event in 1965, following the success of 1964's rally, and indications of wider support. Following these discussions, Bob Wilkinson's and Dave Pullom's offer to undertake and organise social events – which were complementary to the principal road trials and

Tourist Board press release, October 1964. (MNH)

tests – was accepted, along with a proposal to add an extra day, so as to take in two weekends. This plan was rubber-stamped by the Tourist Board in a press release dated October 2, 1964. A further announcement revealed that the Druidale course had been extended to: "50 miles (80.5km) over a wild, mountainous and very testing circuit." Pat Callin, the rally secretary, explained that the number of laps was to increase from three to four, in response to requests from competitors.

Scooter and Three Wheeler magazine suggested that if numbers for the rally continued to fall from a peak of 200 entries in 1959, 1964 might have been the last event if it wasn't for the increase on the previous year, but perhaps more significant was the involvement of Vespa and Lambretta. Bob Wilkinson and Dave Pullom flew to the island in time for the closing stages of the Druidale event, and made a joint announcement at the prize giving ceremony held at Douglas Head. Vice chairman of the rally committee, Eric Coward, claimed that their support might bring 1000 scooterists to the island, and if this target was achieved, Lieutenant Governor Sir Ronald Garvey would present an award to be known as the One Thousand Trophy. It was acknowledged that entry numbers for the 400 and Druidale would be limited, accepted on a first-come, first-served basis. Stan Wardell, clerk to the course, maintained, however, that the rally would not ally itself too closely with any one organisation, and thus lose its independent nature.[52]

Chapter 9

1965: FOR THE RECORD

Mary Black and Anthea Radcliffe, the photograph used on the cover of the official 1965 Rally Programme. (MB)

On May 20, 1965, the front page of the *Examiner* reported a "massive entry for the Scooter Rally," which had exceeded all expectations. Club secretary Pat Callin revealed that although entries had slowed in the last few days, it was still a tremendous figure, which further rose to 384, and included riders from Sweden, Czechoslovakia, Poland, and France. The Sir Ronald Garvey Challenge Cup was to be awarded for the first time to overall winner of the field events, and the Jurby sprint – a new event requested by competitors, for which the rally organisers received 109 entries – was announced for Thursday morning. Friday's Druidale event, with a total distance of 50 miles – described by *Motor Cycling* magazine as "tougher than ever" – was extended from three to four laps, and over-subscribed, with a reserve list of 29 riders.

Last-minute overseas entries, including 11 members of the Vespa Club of Sweden, and a member of the Manet Club of Prague, brought total entries to a record 411, in addition to all of the club members who spectated, meaning that the organiser's hard work of previous years was starting to pay off in terms of worthwhile support.

The first riders arrived on the Friday afternoon, before competitors from the annual International Cycling Week held the previous week had had chance to clear the island. The rest arrived on Saturday with up to a hundred per vessel. At 9am on Sunday morning, the sun broke out of the clouds, shining on "rank upon colourful rank" of scooters as they lined up on the promenade. The weather forecast for the day was 'variable,' and speed warnings were issued for restricted areas such as Bray Hill. At the start of the 400, band leader and race starter Ivy Benson was presented with a bouquet by Jim Cain, who declared that the rally had got off to a good start, not only with the weather but also the record number of entries.[53]

What turned out to be a triumphant week for Vespa began with 24 riders gaining first class awards in the Manx 400, compared to Lambretta's 20. Out of 113

Terry Moore prepares to leave the starting ramp. (TM)

starters there were 90 finishers, with 49 first class awards: a slightly lower percentage than the previous year. Despite Vespa's overall success, rider Ian Kirkpatrick got off to a bad start by losing his time sheet, and was given a 15 point penalty along with a replacement sheet, putting him out of the running for a first or second class award. Another Vespa rider and former champion, John Alexander, was also taken out of the running when his engine seized coming down the mountain section of the TT course. This stretch of road also deprived the previous year's rally champion, Roger Crook, of the chance to repeat his success, when he lost 30 minutes searching for a missing carburettor jet.

A first-time competitor in the Manx 400 was 32-year-old Reverend Peter Turnock from the Wirral, who, despite putting in a faultless performance, picked up three penalty points for lost time caused by a 'tight piston.' Reverend Turnock was a member of Chester Scooter Club, and used his Pacemaker scooter for his parish work. Better

fortune was bestowed upon Polish-born rider Elizabeth Smolen, now of Bebington, Cheshire, who gained a first class award after three years of trying. Four members of the Vespa Club of Sweden achieved first class wards, as did Hans Holzer of Prague, riding a Tartan (a 125cc version of the Manet). Lambretta rider Vic Zealey, from High Wycombe, also gained a first after several attempts.

Three teams completed the event with a clean sheet, including the local Vespa 90s of Ralph Lowey, Alan Killip and Neil Kelly, all riding machines from Gilbert Harding's hire fleet. Other teams comprised the Mancunians (J W Heap and R Mycock), and the Swedish team consisting of G Duell, P Nordberg, and L Henger.[54]

The eagerly-awaited Jurby sprint was the next major event, which took place at the airfield. Eighty-nine machines each made two runs over the ¼ mile (1.21km) course. Fastest rider in the over 200cc class was Malcolm Stevens on his Maico, covering the distance in 20 seconds flat, with timing monitored by flag and stopwatch.

The Druidale event was delayed by 1½ hours due to mist, and although relatively incident-free, the water-splash claimed one victim in the shape of A Barker, plus T F Coleman's Lambretta caught fire just before completion of a lap at Brandywell Cottage. Vespa Sports Club secretary Mike Murphy came out on top on his GS model with a loss of just 122 marks, runners-up being Neil Kelly (Vespa), and H C Watt (Lambretta).

The scramble at Ballacallin attracted a slightly larger entry than in the previous year, with all entries being standard machines. The course was set in the reverse direction this year to avoid a forced narrow turn after a downhill run. Swedish competitors M Eckerstein and P Nordberg came first and second in both the over 150cc and unlimited events, with fellow countryman L Henjer taking first place in the handicap: a particularly impressive result, considering that scooter scrambling is unknown in Sweden.

On Monday evening, competitors and friends were invited to a reception given by the Mayor of Douglas, Cllr J H Moore, at the Villa Marina, at which members of the Swedish team presented him with a pin badge.

Other events included Tuesday's treasure hunt, and the Vespa Club of Britain-hosted evening at the Falcon Cliff Hotel, with parties given by Lambretta club members on Friday, and the Isle of Man Scooter Club on Thursday. The slalom event took place at Onchan Stadium on the Wednesday afternoon; fastest man being Manx 400 first class award winner R T Young from Rutherglen, who completed the course in 31.4 seconds (fastest lady was Elizabeth Smolen).

It was claimed that the 1965 rally was the biggest by far, and believed to have been the best by those who took part. Particular praise was singled out for Kenny Radcliffe, who stepped in to become clerk to the course due to the untimely death of Stan Wardell. Competitors and spectators rose to applaud him at Saturday's prize giving ceremony at Douglas Head Hotel. Reporter Dennis Dalton described the position of clerk to the course as a "stinker" of a job, because "if all goes well, nobody notices. On the other hand, if things go wrong …" The performance of the Swedish competitors was also singled out for special praise, and the hope was expressed that more continental riders would be encouraged to take part in future events.[55]

Vespa Club of Britain members claimed over 50 awards, presented by either the Mayor of Douglas or Mr W E Quayle, chairman of the Tourist Board. Vespa rider Mike Murphy was declared Rally Champion, and collected the Tynwald Challenge Trophy; Elizabeth Smolen was crowned Scooter Queen, and the Vespa 90 team collected the *Scooter and Three Wheeler* challenge

Terry Moore competing at the inaugural Jurby sprint event. (TM)

Swedish competitors presented a pin badge to the Mayor of Douglas. (MNH)

Shield. N A Cooper of Hornchurch won the pre-65 class in the Concours d'Elegance with his 1957 D model Lambretta. Winner of the Scooter Girl competition was Miss M M Walker; the Loving Cup went to Miss Nilsson and Mr G Duell, and sidecar champion was G T W Burnhill for the second successive year.

Chapter 10

1966: WIPEOUT

After all the hard work of making the 1965 rally such a success, with a record number of competitors, things could only get better – it seemed. The 1966 programme shows an entry of over 500 competitors, with international representation from Sweden, Germany, Italy, and Switzerland, and the organisers were ready to capitalise on all the hard work that went into making the previous year's rally a truly world-class event. All that was required was some decent weather ... and transportation to the island, of course. In the year that the TT was postponed until later in the summer, the 1966 Manx International Scooter Rally fell victim to the seamen's strike, and was cancelled altogether.

The Tourist Board was concerned that this should not damage the event's long-term prospects, and sent a publicity team and van to visit scooter rallies throughout England, in order to drum up support for 1967.

Scooter and Three Wheeler correspondent Clive Weavers was asked to report back from the island on the 'Rally that never was,' as printed in the September issue of the magazine. On the Saturday, when most competitors would be travelling to the event, the weather was overcast with occasional showers. Sunday was to have hosted the Manx 400, and although not as bad as on some previous occasions, the rain arrived after lunch with the cloud base becoming lower and lower. Monday saw a break in the bad weather, and was even described as being hot in the afternoon; perfect conditions for the sprint at Jurby airfield, had it happened. A new event – the night navigational trial – was scheduled to begin in 1966, and riders would have been able to "plot their routes under a full moon." The mist returned for Thursday, on which the Druidale race was to have been run, where perfect conditions would have finally prevailed after a possible delay. Clive spoke to a number of local people during the week, who all gave the impression that they had missed the rally.

Lone scooterist at Victoria Pier, taken in 1966, in the week that should have hosted that year's rally. (KR)

Pat Callin polishes the trophies the year that they remained in the cabinet.

Chapter 11

1967: NIGHT TRIAL AND THE RAMSEY SPRINT

Entries for the 1967 event closed on May 20, and totalled 479, including 169 riders for one of that year's inaugural events, the night road trial, five of whom were from Italy and two from Sweden. Upon arrival on the island, the Isle of Man Harbour Board granted permission for fuelling to take place on the pier, to avoid competitors having to congregate at petrol stations with heavily-laden machines.

The first 'Ramsey sprint' along Mooragh promenade was scheduled for Tuesday, with a series of "first class side shows" due to take place in support of the sprint. Scooterists met, as usual, at the informal gathering at the Douglas Head Hotel, with the grand parade leaving the grandstand at 11.15 on Sunday morning.[56] When the late entries were added, the total number of entrants rose to 492, and at 12.00 noon on Sunday, Geoff Duke signalled the start of the Manx 400, during which the competitors endured atrocious weather conditions.

Mrs V Etchells from Oldham lost a point when her time sheet blew away at Goose Neck early in the evening. This section of the mountain course claimed a casualty when 19-year-old Joan Thorne from Bristol crashed her Lambretta, necessitating treatment at Ramsey Cottage Hospital. She completed eight laps without penalty, before writing off her machine on the ninth. Speaking to *Scooter and Three Wheeler* magazine, Joan explained that "I remembered nothing but woke up in hospital."[57] Fortunately, she sustained no serious injuries. It was also reported that Mike Karslake made a "welcome return" to rallying, competing in the sidecar outfit that he used in the Istanbul Rally of 1962. Arthur Francis partnered him in the chair. Amongst the 52 competitors completing the challenging event without penalty was Manxman Terry Moore, competing on his Velocette, the only British scooter entered in the 1967 rally, on which he went on to win the Isle of Man Championship, and was presented with the Wallace Challenge Trophy and a gold award for the 400.

Terry Moore tackles the 400 on the only British-built scooter at the 1967 rally. (TM)

The night trial commenced at 10pm on Monday, June 26, and was described as "a difficult route; resembling that of a car rally." Out of the 90 starters, only 39 completed the course within the time limit. The route was delivered to the competitors at the start line, meaning that solo riders were at a distinct disadvantage, having to stop and plan each section. Experienced trial riders were quick to praise the event, which took place on quiet roads, with emphasis on reading route directions and references. Keith Shaw (Vespa), from Debcross, was declared the victor. The Italian team – eventual winner of the team award – did exceptionally well in this event. It was claimed that one of them did not understand any of the clues on the route card, but said afterwards "I didn't need them."[58]

The Isle of Man Scooter Association Ramsey sprint took place on Tuesday at 1.30pm, with the dual carriageway closed to provide a safe, quarter-mile stretch of road. Conditions were good, and although some spectators lined the route, many chose to watch the proceedings through the windows of their bed and breakfast lodgings. The winner of the sidecar event was Arthur Francis from Croxley Green, coming in at 26.31 seconds in the 170cc class, and Mike Karslake triumphed in the over-170cc class combination. First in the solo 125cc class was Bob Jackson at 21.13 seconds, with I F Willingham, also from Bradford, coming in at 16.75 seconds in the 200cc class. In the over 200cc class, Miss J M Lloyd from Hampton recorded a time of 19.99 seconds.

Amongst the field events on Wednesday was the mock TT race, held on a grass field laid out in a circle, and incorporating a running jump and straw bales, in an attempt to avoid which, one machine came a cropper. As helpers rushed to his aid, fellow competitor Gordon Roper appeared at speed to see six spectators with their backs to him, oblivious to his approach. The ensuing collision left George horizontal on the grass, along with the spectators. The clerk to the course suffered a broken leg in another incident, whilst Norman Ronald became embroiled in a four-way crash. Neville Frost was forced into retirement, allowing R A Froud, the eventual Field Events Champion, to win by a whisker, with John Forster in hot pursuit. The climax to the pram race came on the 9th lap, when Mike Karslake, swinging widely, turned the outfit on its side. Mike tumbled out gently, but his passenger, Arthur Francis, "did a neat dive over the lot, landing on his head." Arthur did, however, make a quick recovery, in time for a lap of honour, to the "delighted applause of the crowd."

Accusations were made that Thursday's Druidale was the "dullest ever," and heavily loaded in favour of the Italians' 125cc Special Lambrettas which were not yet available in Britain. The laps were timed, and the timing strip was located just below the hairpin at Brandywell. The Italian riders arrived well ahead of time and halted on the far side, keeping a keen eye on the stopwatch. They were then able to start their engines and pass the line dead on time. It was stated that all scooters should be racing

Right: Terry Moore is rewarded with the Watsonian Challenge Cup for his success in the 1967 rally. (TM)

Unrelated, but collectively known as 'The Flying Moore's' are (from left to right) Norman Moore, Peter Curphey, Les and Terry Moore. (LM)

against the clock for the entire race, rather than hanging about, waiting.[59]

In brilliant sunshine on Friday, the motocross event took place, over a short but bumpy and hilly circuit littered with many obstacles, including rocks and gorse. The finish line was preceded by a bumpy slope and corner. Classes consisted of up to 150cc; unlimited; a race for non-winners of these two, and, finally, an invitational race. Every rider had to complete a practice lap first, during which Elizabeth Smolen suffered a bad crash, causing a rope burn to her face. Lap speeds were around 47-48 seconds, and despite receiving a nudge, Neville Frost was fastest man in the unlimited cc class. The final of the 150cc class saw a solid start by Luke Kitto and R Froud, the latter dropping his machine on lap four. After a close battle with M Braithwaite, Froud eventually came in second, 14.75 seconds behind winner Luke Kitto.

The prize giving ceremony duly took place at Douglas Head Hotel, the presentations made by the Lieutenant Governor, Sir Peter Stallard, and the Mayor of Douglas, James Callister. This year's Rally Champion and winner of the Premier Award was John Ronald of Nottingham (Lambretta), which was presented with a replica of the Tynwald Challenge Trophy and £15 in prize money. Elizabeth Smolen (Vespa) retained the title of Scooter Queen, winning the Power and Pedal Challenge Trophy and £10. Best sidecar and winner of the Watsonian

Challenge Trophy went to G T W Burnhill and passenger M Adams (Vespa). The Senior Druidale event was won by Italian rider Giorgio Sicbaldi (Lambretta), with the Junior award going to Luke Kitto (Vespa) from Exeter. The team award and the Sir Ronald Garvey Challenge Cup, plus £12 in prize money, was claimed by the Lambretta Club d'Italia, consisting of Giorgio Sicbaldi, B Appolloni, and A Paggi. Best Scooter was awarded to N T Kemp (Vespa) from Luton.

During the presentation ceremony, clerk to the course Kenny Radcliffe claimed that the TT race was held on the scooter course, and not the other way around, much to the approval of the audience.[60] Joan Thorne recovered from her accident to win the Scooter Girl competition, and the Loving Cup was presented to Miss J Cotterill and Mr B Harris from Northampton, all three of whom were shortly to be married. Douglas director Eric Brockway filled the Loving Cup with champagne, and this was duly passed round by Vespa Club of Britain secretary Ian Kirkpatrick. *Scooter and Three Wheeler* concluded that, with the exception of Druidale, it had been a "wonderful week."

For a full listing & details of all our titles please visit – www.veloce.com
All current books • New book news • Special offers • Gift vouchers • Forum

73

Chapter 12

On May 30, 1968, the *Examiner* reported a "massive" record entry for the forthcoming rally, with 190 for the Manx 400, 160 for the night trial, 158 for Druidale, 144 for the Ramsey sprint, 81 for the motocross, 85 for the new sand race, and 531 for the gymkhana-type field events. Five Italians were set to defend their team award, with Giorgio Sicbaldi hoping to replicate his success as fastest man over Druidale.

Giorgio began his riding career on Vespas back in 1960, but in 1964 he became a member of the official Lambretta team, and was selected to represent Lambretta in the Isle of Man Rally. J C Breggazi was to preside as chairman for the first time, with Paul Martin appointed rally steward by the Federation of British Scooter Clubs. In the foreword to the 1968 programme, Mr Bregazzi said he was delighted to welcome scooterists to the Isle of Man, stating that the programme had been developed to suit all tastes, with events including the Manx '400,' Ramsey sprint, night trial, Druidale, motocross, and sand racing, together with less strenuous activities such as the treasure hunt, field events, conducted tours and social evenings. An innovation for '68 was the award of the ScotManx Trophy for best performance by a member of the Scottish Scooter Clubs Association, the actual cup provided by Messrs Allan, Barbour, and Young.

The final number of competitors for the 1968 Manx 400 stood at 192, of which there were 31 retirements and 31 non-starters. The riders left the starting ramp, positioned outside the Sefton Hotel, at 12.00 noon. The Glen Helen checkpoint was kept open all day, but all riders took a compulsory 30-minute stop between 6pm and 8.30pm, during which time their scooters were impounded. The checkpoint at the grandstand operated on a permanent basis, with all major repairs being undertaken in the pit area, with event control, Castrol, Lambretta and Vespa servicing all operating in the area. Other checkpoints were operating at Kirk Michael, Quarry

Rider 501, Derrick Shimmin, carries out some essential repairs. (IOMSC)

Verner tackles the night trial. (MNH)

Pram races at Noble's Park. Rider 478 is J E Gasson, with George Pearce in the pram. (MNH)

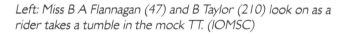

Left: Miss B A Flannagan (47) and B Taylor (210) look on as a rider takes a tumble in the mock TT. (IOMSC)

Bends, Goose Neck, North Barrule, and Creg ny-Baa, and opened and closed at the organisers' discretion.[61]

A total of 102 gold awards were given, with 21 silver and nine bronze. One of the silver awards went to Isle of Man Scooter Club captain Colin Skillicorn for the second year running (he lost points due to electrical failure).

A broken wire in the electrics also caused the retirement of Frank Carter, and B Roscoe's participation was curtailed by a broken wrist. Doug Saunders was forced out, having suffered a broken tooth in his gearbox, and a failed throttle cable meant that Pete Trulock had to settle for a silver award. Manxman Les Moore experienced fuel trouble when a fibre washer broke up and fouled the fuel pipes, and Bob McFee was forced to retire after nine laps due to the recurring effects of a past injury. Terry Moore was presented with a fifth consecutive gold award for the Manx 400, and, along with Norman Moore and Malcolm Black, received the Master Scooterist Shield: a new award, open to all competitors who began the week by riding in the '400.' To receive this award (a lapel badge with year bars), riders had to complete all checks in the night trial, obtain at least a bronze in the 400, and complete the Druidale event.

The Ramsey sprint was held on Monday, with a funfair in attendance and the road closed to normal traffic. Ron Moss was the fastest man, recording a time of 18.9 seconds; K Web was second with 19 seconds, and John Ronald came third with 19.3 seconds, the top three finishing way out in front, although unable to break Fred Willingham's 1967 record of 16.75 seconds.

The night trial began on Tuesday evening with 140 riders tackling 80 miles (128.75km) of terrain which ranged from first class roads to country tracks. Machines were flagged off from the grandstand at one-minute intervals. Only 84 machines completed the trial, leaving the Manx countryside littered with broken-down scooters. Competitor Allen Grey 'ran out of track' and wrote off his Lambretta, twisting the frame. One of the competitors was 1967 All-Britain Scooter Champion Neville Frost from London: he finished in second place behind Malcolm Lake, who completed the course with a loss of just 17 points. Interviewed in 2012, Malcolm Black recalled that he was a travelling marshal at this event. Approached by three competitors, all from London, who had become lost during the small hours of the morning at the Curraghs, behind the Wildlife Park, Malcom offered to lead them back onto the correct route, around a sharp right-hand turn next to a deep ditch full of water, into which, all three competitors rode! Malcolm declined the offer of also becoming waist-deep in water to help retrieve the scooters, opting, instead, to wait for the pick-up

Members of the Eastleigh Hornets compete in the night trial. (IOMSC)

truck. The unfortunate victims relayed the event to him at the presentation awards ceremony, fortunately not recognising Malcolm, who noted that they never returned to the island!

Thursday's Druidale event was delayed by mist, but when the sun finally broke through at 11am, the first rider – Mike Pierce – was flagged off, with the rest dispatched at 30-second intervals. Brenda Surry from Enfield came to grief within two miles, and Liz Smolen, this year teamed up with Nickspeed, went over a wall just before the water-splash, although, amazingly, managed to continue, despite knocking herself out! Rider Paul Laskey collided with a sign at a bad left-hander, but also managed to continue, despite bending his forks.

A rider becomes airborne during the motocross event. (IOMSC)

Norman Ronald of Team S Equipe; fastest man in the Druidale event. (IOMSC)

Crowds gather for the 1968 sand races. (IOMSC)

Championship hopeful Neville Frost lost time on the water-splash section, ruling him out of the Premier Award.[62] Italian R Ferri came in 4th, although would have been in contention for first place if he hadn't dropped his Lambretta on the first lap. Team colleague Georgio Sicbaldi, despite winning the Senior Druidale in 1967, was forced to settle for a place in the Junior event this year, following his performance in the 400 and the night trial.

Scootering and Lightweights magazine commented on the officials' estimate of between three and five thousand spectators for the sand racing event: "They were there to see – and hear." it said. *Mona's Herald* put crowd numbers even higher at 6000, but whatever the correct number, all of them cheered throughout the two-hour event. The track was described as "a bit treacherous" for the first lap as the tide had left the sand rippled, but gave way over subsequent laps to allow controlled drifting, even for solo riders. K Shaw from Oldham (Vespa) won the 100cc class; A Flack from Sheffield (Vespa) the up to 150cc, and in the over 150cc solos J B Stockport (Lambretta) was victorious. First in the unlimited invitational solo race was M Braithwaite from Hale (Vespa).

There were two sidecar classes; first in the scratch race were Geoff Burnhill and A Williams from London (Vespa), and the winners of the sidecar handicap race

77

Left to right: D Wenham, P J Yates, and JN Jones are the riders in the driving seat competing at Douglas sand races. (MNH)

Mike Karslake in 1968's sand races held on Douglas beach. (MNH)

were D Wenham from Littlehampton, and P Hall from Seaford (Vespa.)

Club secretary Pat Callin declared the rally a tremendous success, with 531 the official number of entries. Pat revealed that, before leaving on Sunday, 203 of the competitors had paid to participate in the following year's competition.[63]

The Premier Award and Tynwald Trophy were presented to John Ronald of Birmingham for the second successive year, with Norman Ronald and Nev Frost finishing in 2nd and 3rd places overall. Repeat success was also achieved by Elizabeth Smolen, Lady Champion for the third successive year, which meant she got to keep the trophy. Sidecar champion was J N F Jones (Lambretta) with his passenger, N Banks from Liverpool. The Team Award was convincingly won by Team S Equipe, and the IOM Championship and Wallace Trophy was retained by Terry Moore. R McKay of Aberdeen (Vespa) was declared Best Scottish Rider; Peter Chapman (Vespa) came out on top in the field events; Rally Champion John Ronald was fastest man over Druidale, with Italian Giorgio Sicbaldi winning the Junior Druidale section, and R Ferri, also from the Italian team, awarded Best Lambretta Newcomer. Malcolm Stevens won the Maico Challenge Cup, and Luke Kitto won the Vespa Challenge Trophy.

Allegations of 'professionalism' were levelled against John and Norman Ronald, and their Team S Equipe colleague, Neville Frost, but they had built their own machines without any backing from any of the manufacturers' teams, and the trio were robustly and rightly defended in *Scooter and Lightweights* magazine. A huge amount of preparation and planning went into preparing the scooters, and the logic of paying to enter races and then not doing their utmost to win was obviously questionable.[64] Speaking to *Scooter World*, John Ronald explained that: "We've spent hours in preparation. That's when you get results." Their Lambrettas were stock machines using carburettors from the 200cc model, opened-up transfer ports, close-ratio gears, and an enlarged exhaust manifold, and were the culmination of years of research.[65]

A retrospective look at these allegations reveals that these machines were prepared by dedicated individuals, not manufacturer teams. The serious racing element that began to establish itself as part of Scootering Week in the late 1960s was, arguably, what enabled it to continue for as long as it did.

John Ronald receives the Tynwald Trophy for the second time. (IOMSC)

For a full listing & details of all our titles please visit – www.veloce.com
All current books • New book news • Special offers • Gift vouchers • Forum

79

Chapter 13

1969: KING OF THE HILL

A record number of competitors continued to congregate on the island in 1969, with entries for the Manx 400 topping 200 for the first time, taking the rally entry total to 534. Entries were up for all events except the sand race, as participation in this was 'on the spot.'

The Manx 400 was started at 10.30am by Leonard Bond, secretary of the Isle of Man Tourist Board, in fantastic weather conditions. Andre Baldet marked his return after a five-year absence by competing in a sidecar outfit with his wife as passenger. An all-girl sidecar crew consisted of Jennie Stevens and Miss K Lawrence (Maico). John Ronald lined up to try and make it a rally champion hat trick: not yet achieved in the event's history. Mike Karslake, having gone to great effort to overhaul

Competitors line up for the 1969 Manx 400. (MNH)

Continued page 97

Lambretta rally control van.

Castrol service van.

Czechoslovak Ultra-Lightweights on the Tourist Trophy Course

Fully fashioned — First at the Concours d'elegance and then on the renowned Tourist Trophy course — this time with Eddie Crooks at the controls of the 50 c. c. Jawa.

J. ALEXANDER, Liverpool

Only a few days after the successful appearance of František Šťastný with his CZ 350 Jawa, the renowned T.T. course with all its hazards was brought to life once more. This time it was invaded by a multitude of scooters of all well known makes, which had been entered to prove their endurance and reliability in the toughest event ever devised for them.

The Manx 400 — that is what they call the scooter battle held in the Isle of Man — proud island which stands for the past, present, and let us hope also the future of motor cycling. The machines have to complete a given number of laps on the circuit (which is almost 38 miles in length), depending on their engine capacity. Scooters in the 100 c. c. class had to complete 12 laps. This amounts to an average of ... m. p. h. — a really tough proposition on such an arduous circuit.

The position of Eddie Crooks and Roger Kelly, both of whom had appeared on the entry lists of several International Six Days' Trials in connection with machines of Czechoslovak origin. As anything but enviable. As there was no 50 c. c. class, these courageous sportsmen astride Jawa 05 machines with a capacity of 50 c. c. faced competition from mounts of twice that capacity in the 100 c. c. class which they were forced to enter by circumstances. The weather was not going

to be good and during weighing-in the Clerk of the Course, Mr. S. Wardell, read a discouraging weather forecast for the morning of the following day when the start was scheduled at 9 a. m. Things turned out as bad as expected. After a night of heavy rain, there was drizzle and fog on the Mountain.

There was fog from Guthries Memorial to Keppel Gate and visibility was down to 50 yards or less. Roads were slippery at Sulby Bridge and worst of all, the greatest enemy of lightweights, a strong wind — blew high at the highest point on the course near East Snaefell Gate.

Both the Jawa 05 lightweights were handicapped by being pitted against machines of twice their capacity and additionally, they were in standard trim. This made a big contrast with their more powerful rivals, often relying on the help of special gear boxes with eight or ten ratios. On top of all this, both riders who rode Jawa fives tip the scales at more than 12 stone, to which must be added the weight of their cumbersome riding kit needed to counter bad weather. Thus they entered the fray against great odds, relying only on their own riding experience and on their faith in the staying power of the tiny mounts.

At seven minutes past nine, Eddie Crooks was sent off and a few minutes later Roger

The Green Flag reported that the 1964 Isle of Man Scooter Rally had received worldwide publicity, featuring in the Czechoslovak publication Motor Review, which detailed the exploits of two of the rally's "oustanding" motorcyclists – Eddie Crooks and Roger Kelly – in the previous year's Manx 400. Also pictured were Eddie and his wife – and Scooter Girl winner – Pauline.

Cover pictures come from the Isle of Man, visited by the Editor on a 350 Jawa. The port of Douglas is on the front page. At the other end of this issue, you will find Point of Ayre lighthouse, on the northernmost tip of Manx. Inside cover pages portray the atmosphere of this year's tough International Six Days' Trial.

Published by RAPID, Praha 1, ul. 28, řijna 13, Czechoslovakia ● Editorial and Publishing Office, Praha 1, ulice 28. řijna 13, Phone 25-11-61, Czechoslovakia ● Published twelve times a year in English, French, German, Spanish and Russian ● Editorial Board: Jaroslav Procházka – Chairman, Vladimír Haveau, Jaroslav Rešil, Ladislav Krahulík, Mirko Kubeš, Karel Pašinek, Josef Počba, Jiři Pawrasník, Vladimír Sekal, Karel Růžička – Editor ● Printed by Středočeské tiskárny, zór. 194, Praha 1, Myslíkova 15

VOL. 9

CZECHOSLOVAK
Motor Review

11
1963

Copyright reserved. Articles may be reprinted whole or in part if the source is quoted as: Czechoslovak Motor Review. Contributions received by the editorial office are not returned.

The annual subscription rate for twelve issues amounts to 4 Dollars (US), or their equivalent in the currency of the country of destination. The exact amount in any currency can be learned from our circulation department, enquiries should be addressed: RAPID, ul. 28, řijna 13, Praha 1, Czechoslovakia. Remittances through State banks československé. Account 2F/22, cheques etc. must be marked "Motor Review subscription". Agents: Britain: Collets Holdings, Ltd., 44—45 Museum Street London W. C. 1, USA: Stecher-Hafner Inc., 31, East 10th Str. New York 3, N. Y. Canada: Davies Book Company Ltd., 5030 Melrose Ave., Montreal. Australia: Current Book Distributors, 40, Market Street, Sydney, N. S. W. India: Fort, Bombay 1. Japan: Nauka Ltd., Current Book House, P.O. Box 1007i, 32 Kanda Zinbocho, Chiyoda-Ku, Tokyo.

Malcolm Black checks in at the grandstand. (MB)

Terry Moore makes his usual spectacular entry to the water-splash at Druidale. (TM)

Right: 1968 programme.

THE ELEVENTH ISLE OF MAN

SCOOTER
HOLIDAY WEEK

Photograph by courtesy of W. H. Heaps

1968

22 - 29 JUNE

ISLE OF MAN

DOUGLAS   ISLE OF MAN

ISLE OF MAN MOTOR SCOOTER ASSOCIATION

This is to Certify that

P.R.G. Bargery

has completed the

NIGHT ROAD TRIAL

which was run on June 25 1968

with the loss of 65 marks

J. P. CALLIN, Secretary of the Meeting

Peter Bargery night road trial, 1968.

Norman Ronald at the Ramsey sprint. (NR)

Combination team Jenny Stevens and Les Moore on the mountain section. (LM)

Kathleen Westaway competing in the Concours d'Elegance.
(IOMSC)

THIRTEENTH
Isle of Man
SCOOTER
HOLIDAY
WEEK

Photograph by courtesy of W. H. Heaps.

1970

20 · 27 JUNE

1970 programme.

SCOOTERMANIA!

Left: Jim Chappell tackles the Peel hill climb, pictured here at around the halfway section. (IOMSC)

Above: Jenny and Les hit the water-splash at Druidale ... (LM)

... negotiate Brack-a-Broom ... (LM)

... and contend with the sharp left-hander. (LM)

1972 full day trial, and full day trial reverse sheet.

Norrie Kerr at Druidale. (NK)

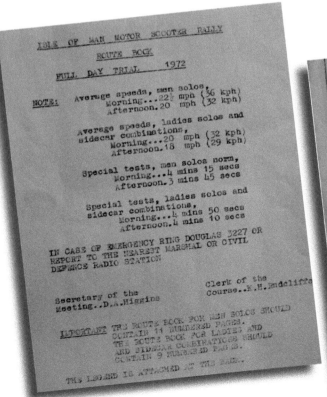

ISLE OF MAN MOTOR SCOOTER RALLY

ROUTE BOOK

FULL DAY TRIAL 1972

NOTE: Average speeds, men solos,
Morning...22½ mph (36 kph)
Afternoon.20 mph (32 kph)

Average speeds, ladies solos and
sidecar combinations,
Morning...20 mph (32 kph)
Afternoon.18 mph (29 kph)

Special tests, men solos norm,
Morning...4 mins 15 secs
Afternoon.3 mins 45 secs

Special tests, ladies solos and
sidecar combinations,
Morning...4 mins 50 secs
Afternoon.4 mins 10 secs

IN CASE OF EMERGENCY RING DOUGLAS 3227 OR
REPORT TO THE NEAREST MARSHAL OR CIVIL
DEFENCE RADIO STATION

Secretary of the   Clerk of the
Meeting..D.A.Higgins   Course..E.H.Radcliffe

IMPORTANT THE ROUTE BOOK FOR MEN SOLOS SHOULD
CONTAIN 11 NUMBERED PAGES.
THE ROUTE BOOK FOR LADIES AND
AND SIDECAR COMBINATIONS SHOULD
CONTAIN 9 NUMBERED PAGES.

THIS LEGEND IS ATTACHED AT THE BACK.

FULL DAY TRIAL NAVIGATION LEGEND

SYMBOLS:
Major Road   Bridge   Lake or Sea
Minor Road   River   Gate
Stone Track   Railway   Church
Green Lane   Plantation   House etc.

(1) Start from the bottom of each picture at "O" and
work up to the arrow for the correct direction.
(2) Where no mileage is given the next instruction
will be obvious.
(3) Where a mileage is given, it is the distance
between consecutive pictures therefore any
side roads must be ignored. (Note: Kilo
equivalents are in brackets)
(4) Where it is thought necessary for clarity, the
direction indicated by signposts will be written
in the space under each picture.

EXAMPLE: ....proceed along major road then,
(at picture A) turn RIGHT onto minor road
crossing bridge over stream, then (B) turn RIGHT
at major road then LEFT onto stone track signposted Ramsey. Follow obvious main track for
0.7 (seven tenths of a mile or 1.1 kilos) then
(C) bear RIGHT onto green lane and Fo through
gate into plantation then (D) turn RIGHT at main
road by Church then LEFT at roundabout and cross
railway lines ....

87

SCOOTERMANIA!

Above: Gold award for the Manx 400.

Right: The Villiers Trophy.

Above: Manxman Terry Moore's impressive trophy haul, rally and Scooter Club awards.

The surviving Lambretta which belonged to rally marshal and IOM Scooter Club member Arthur Garrett.

Manchester Lions Scooter Club entrant.

June Stirrup.

Flat out: rider unknown.

Liz Chappell receives her award. (IOMSC)

Vespa club members celebrate their success. (IOMSC)

1 Keith Shaw
2 Sheila Thomas
3 Steve Hanlon
4 Luke Kitto
5 Alan Hudson
6 Jim Neil
7 Steve Roberts
8 Liz Chappell
9 Jim Chappel
10 Kenny Radcliffe
11 Norrie Kerr
12 Duncan McKenzie

Andy Smith, winner of the Tynwald Trophy. (IOMSC)

Scooter Queen of 1975, Liz Chappell: a member of Avon Valley Scooter Club, Bristol.

Don Browning's combination Lambretta. (NK)

Andy and Pauline Smith, winners of the 1975
Premier Award. (NK)

1975 programme.

1975
ISLE OF MAN
HOLIDAY RALLY
FOR
MOTORCYCLES
AND SCOOTERS

- Programme
  of Events
- Supplementary
  Regulations
- Entry Form

A NEWTON.

Ted and Lesley Parrott from Torbay. (NK)

Riders assemble at the Tholt-y-Will Inn, 1976. (MNH)

1 Terry Frankland 2 John Illing 3 Nigel Ashbrook 4 Pauline Smith 5 Colin Hart
6 Ted Carter 7 Iggy Prackauskas 8 Jim Neil 9 Jenny Stevens 10 Rick Simpson 11 Steve Marsay

1976 social event ticket.

№ 86

ISLE OF MAN HOLIDAY RALLY ASSOCIATION
27 AUBURN ROAD, ONCHAN

Receipt for 50p. Advanced Social Entry and Ticket for Draw of £50 towards 1976 Isle of Man Holiday Rally Week.

(Payable during 1976 Holiday Week).

Signed **DAVID A. HIGGINS,**
(Secretary).

V.P. LTD.

Isle of Man Scooter Club Peel ride-out, July 2013.
(Author collection)

Manx National Heritage
Eiraght Ashoonagh Vannin

Concours d'Elegance, Villa Marina.

Pat Callin looks at the stopwatch as the flag comes down. (MNH)

Riders emerge from the Bungalow on the TT course. (MNH)

his Lambretta sidecar outfit, was forced to retire on the second lap. Close inspection revealed that the fault was nothing more than an HT lead which had been cut too short, and was working loose inside the suppressor cap.[66] Gold awards were claimed by 75 of the 202 starters, along with 18 silver and 18 bronze. Golds went to 1968's Total Championship of Sweden winner Rutger Moller and fellow Swede Frimann Clausen. Norrie Kerr, J W and Mrs Clark, T J Tobin, D W Bain and Gordon Roper (all Vespa), and Tommy Steel (Lambretta) all secured gold awards, making 1969 a hugely successful year for Scottish riders. Amongst the silver winners were Bob Mcfee from Onchan, and Peter Cain from Douglas, with local rider Norman Moore achieving bronze success. Alan Mills from Rochdale received cuts and bruises when his machine was involved in a collision with a van at Ballaugh Bridge.

A new speed climb event was held on Monday evening – the 'King of the Hill' Trophy for the fastest machine up Peel Hill, which overlooks the harbour – presented by Peel Town Commissioners. There were 200 competitors for this event, cheered on by a large crowd of spectators. The course was described in *Scooter World*

Pete Hasler at the first Peel hill climb competition. (MNH)

1969 night trial. (IOMSC)

Field events get under way. (IOMSC)

Scrutineering controversy. (MNH)

as having a "tricky start followed by a slogging climb." In the sidecar class, last year's overall winner, J N F Jones (Liverpool Sporting Club), retired with a burned-out clutch. Although Jones recorded the fastest time, the honours went to Geoff Burnhill (Vespa) as the result rested on both runs. The solo machines of Gordon Roper and Ron Moss proved quick, and Ian Calder from Rochdale notched up fastest time (53.4 seconds). His second run was off the pace, unfortunately, and Colin Prior of the Eastleigh

Hornets was outright winner with fastest time of the day at 52 seconds.

The night semi-sporting trial was flagged off at 9pm, still in daylight, from the grandstand on Tuesday evening. The organisers kept the course a closely-guarded secret, with riders having just a sketched route map to guide them. Amongst the starters was Dot Hasler from Twickenham on a Vespa 90 SS, boosted to 125cc to facilitate husband Peter as pillion and navigator.

Top: Nev Frost at the Douglas sand races, which still drew the crowds in '69. (IOMSC)

Above: Scooter Girl line-up. (IOMSC)

Right: Scooter Girl winner, Kathleen Westaway. (IOMSC)

Sixty-two-year-old H A Dudley was competing in his fifth consecutive Manx Rally, having just missed out on a gold in this year's 400. It was remarked on that this competition was becoming the most difficult event, after just 57 riders completed the course. Fortunes were mixed, and many lost their way at some point. John Ronald was observed "belting towards the checkpoint, but approaching in the wrong direction."[67] Rutger Moller was forced into retirement after seven miles with a blown rectifier, and H J Tobin was on the pace right until the last two miles when he hit a boulder, dropping him from a high placing to 54th. Dave Purrington (Exeter Yokels) also suffered from bent forks, and Gordon Roper ran out of fuel.

It was a good night for the Torbay team, with Keith Shaw, Ted Parrott and Roy Owens all getting gold awards. The winner, with a loss of just 12 points, was R T (Bob) Young of East Kilbride, and Dot Hasler made it a one-two for Vespa as first lady to finish: a result which earned her the title of Scooter Queen. Terry Moore was amongst the finishers, following his gold award in the 400, continuing his impressive run of rally success. Although it was a tough course, including 10 miles (16.1km) of green lanes, no serious injuries or accidents were reported, although most competitors parted company with their machines at some point during the 4-hour event.

The fine weather continued, ensuring a large crowd for Wednesday's gymkhana events; the mock TT again creating a lot of interest. Norrie Kerr, having dropped his Vespa, seemed more concerned about his bike than his own welfare. A reporter stood in place at the starting ramp, but reportedly fled to safety as the scooters hit the ramp at speed. This year, riders were compelled to remove their side panels to prevent them from flying off. Many riders were de-seated in the mayhem that was the mock TT, though, fortunately, only minor injuries resulted. Keith Shaw led the field for a large part of the race, but was overtaken on the last stretch by eventual winner Alan Crickmore from Southampton. *Scooter World* reported that some of the top riders were notable by their absence, suggesting that events such as this should be linked to the Premier Award, thus encouraging participation.[68]

Despite the bright sunshine that greeted the start of the rally, Druidale was blighted by thick mist and heavy rain, forcing officials to delay the start of the time trial by over an hour. Despite visibility being restricted to 100 metres, clerk to the course Norman Corlett declared that racing would begin at 11.15am, although riders were asked to proceed with caution for the initial lap.

First man away was P C Clutton of the Laughing Cavaliers Scooter Club, in weather which fluctuated between mist and rain. A 'Slow Down' sign was erected just after the timed section at Brandywell, much to the disappointment of the spectators. After two laps, competitors and officials alike had had enough, and the race was abandoned, with the results based on the two completed laps. The Druidale Junior event was cancelled outright.

A row erupted during the scrutineering which followed, when Ron Moss was disqualified for having an oversize barrel of 200.8796cc. Protests were immediately lodged, as the piston was a genuine Lambretta part, albeit a third oversize for a 200cc machine. Later discovered to be commonly used in federation events, and permitted under the general competition rules, the piston was allowed, enabling Ron to finish 4th overall in the 1969 rally.[69]

On the Thursday evening riders enjoyed a BBQ organized by the Isle of Man Scooter Club Ladies Committee.

Overall champion for 1969 was 32-year-old engine tester Peter Chapman from Coventry, who lost only 161 points throughout the competition, competing in his fourth IOM Scooter Week. John Ronald was denied his third win, finishing in seventh place. Sidecar Champion was Geoff Burnhill. The award ceremony took place at the Majestic Hotel, and the prizes were presented by the Mayor, C E Burke, a member of the Scooter Association Committee. Scooter Queen and Lady Champion Dot Hasler was presented with the Challenge Award in the design of a crown, donated by Elizabeth Smolen when she retained the Challenge Cup after her hat trick of wins in 1968. Miss Kathleen Westaway of Torquay won the Scooter Girl contest, and Loving Cup winners were Swedish pair Miss Anne Ortefors and Jens Clausen, secretary of the Vespa Club of Gothenburg.

In the September issue of *Scooter World* Kenny Radcliffe, speaking on behalf of the Isle of Man Rally Association, shared his thoughts on what he described as a "difficult year," largely due to there being a different clerk to the course for every event, and the fact that too much officialdom was creeping into the organisation: the regulations now so cumbersome that few fully understood them, leading to "confusion and bitterness." Radcliffe stressed his intention to urge for a complete redraft of these, and also acknowledged the widening gap between the expert rider and the club scooterist riding on a tight budget, for which he had drafted a new deal for the clubman and youngsters to whom the rally depended for the majority of events. An editorial comment was added to the article, which suggested that the field events should count toward the Overall Award, as many riders opted out of these. It was also suggested that only those models of scooter that were generally available should be permitted, and it was asked at what level should works support cease?

The Team Nickspeed combo crew. (MNH)

Chapter 14

1970: RALLY IN PERIL

Despite the record number of competitors at the 1969 event, unfortunately, this momentum did not continue into the new decade. Immediately after the rally, several riders committed to attend in 1970, and it was hoped that the success of '69 would be repeated. However, the May issue of *Scooter World* magazine disclosed that the proposed 1970 programme had been met with a "vociferous barrage of criticism," the organisers commenting it had been drawn to their attention that there were too many events, denying competitors the time needed to repair and maintain their machines; to rest, or simply enjoy the Island. Consequently, a more compact programme was drawn up in which the Manx 400 was combined with Monday's full day trial, the only difference being that circuits would not last more than half a day. It was also claimed that if this drastic reorganisation and reduction in the number of events had not taken place, not a single official would have had anything to do with the 1970 event: the new programme was the only alternative to the complete abandonment of Scooter Week, it seemed. In addition to the full day trial, the surviving competitive events were the Peel hill climb on Tuesday, Druidale on Thursday, and the sand races on Friday, prior to the prize giving ceremony.

The rally secretary added that, with five weeks to go, organisers were "somewhat disturbed" by the low number of entries. Whilst the record entries of 1969 were not expected due to the change of programme, letters from scooterists suggested that there was a general movement to boycott the rally, in the belief that this would force a return to the original programme in time for 1971. Pat Callin warned that this would 'boomerang' on scooterists, because if the 1970 event was poorly attended, and had to be cancelled, there would not be an event in 1971 or any other year. It was pointed out that the committee received generous support from the Isle of Man government, but that it "would not subscribe to something

that was not going to be supported. No 1970 – no future." Callin finished by urging scooterists to submit their entry as their last chance to keep scootering on the TT course or anywhere else on the island.

The 1970 event did take place in the end, albeit with smaller numbers, and the majority of the week was blessed with fine weather. For the first time all competitors – under a new ruling of the Federation of British Scooter Clubs – were required to be covered by a special licence costing 5 shillings per year. It was explained that, in events where speed was the governing factor, necessary precautions had to be taken for insurance purposes.[70]

Scooter World magazine was present with microphone and camera, and spoke to Anne Weir from Manchester about her gold award in the full day trial: "The night trial was only four hours' duration at 20mph (32.2kph); it didn't seem long. The route-finding was not difficult, though I did go wrong once. I think that the points I lost were from booking in too early at the checkpoint. On the tarmac sections the riders were dawdling, waiting for the time to pass. You lose twice as many points booking in early as you do booking in late." Anne added that her clutch plate failed on the hill climb, and that the engine on her Lambretta SX 150 was not running too well, which had only 571 miles on the clock prior to the rally. She claimed to have enjoyed the barbecue, but missed out on the free beer.[71] Anne was one of five women competitors to win a gold medal at the 1970 event.

Tom Croxton was declared winner of the full day trial, which consisted of seven laps of the TT course, followed by the 80 mile (128.75km) navigational test, in which he lost only 11 marks. Tom was a technician at the Luton College of Further Education, and his club colleague, Bert Dudley, aged 63, was the oldest competitor at the rally. Les Moore was teamed up with Jenny Stevens in the sidecar, and recalled this event when interviewed in 2012: they came across a pair of boots in the middle of the road

Rider 52, Gordon Roper, and rider 75, Bob Young, compete on an off-road section of the full day trial. (MNH)

at Bishops Court, which belonged to Mike Karslake. He had been forced to retire, and this was his signal to let them know that he was okay.

The fine weather didn't hold out for the barbecue and the Peel climb, which proved too much for all but one of the sidecar outfits, with Jenny and Les the only riders to reach the top on the Maico. Jenny, from Tolworth in Surrey, currently held third position in the British Scooter Track Championship, and was attending her fifth rally on the Isle of Man. The course had some difficult corners, and was covered with humped-back mounds. Using a clutch start, riders were faced with a sharp uphill stretch, which quickly levelled out before the real climb began to the top of the hill, 600 feet (182.88m) above sea level; they

had also to contend with heavy rain and wind blowing in from the sea. John Forster from Stockport won the solo event, completed two runs, each in less than one minute, and came third in the senior Druidale event.

Good weather returned for the Senior Druidale, with only two riders losing less than 50 penalty points. S Gray from Stirling was forced into retirement after the initial lap: "In the Druidale, there's this long straight. I was doing about 70mph flat out, and there were these sheep in the road. I missed the sheep but I hit the hedge; only bruises to me, but that's why there's no air filter but just a bit of rag tucked into the air inlet. The scooter wasn't a runner after that so I didn't finish."

Geoff Burnhill crashed at the last corner of the circuit,

delaying the start of the junior event as the ambulance was called out to take him to the hospital suffering from a dislocated elbow, cuts and bruises. The other ambulance stationed at Brandywell was also in use, taking Haydn Redfern from Leicester to hospital after his crash at the water-splash.[72]

Friday played host to the popular sand races on Douglas beach, watched by large numbers of holidaymakers. The track was marked out with oil drums, and riders completed a practice lap before being grouped into their various classes. With the big machines, the lead was passed between John Forster, Gordon Roper, and P C Meads. Meads led in one heat but pushed too hard and dropped his machine, though re-started and finished that lap in third place. John Forster won the event overall with Gordon Roper coming in second. Interviewed afterwards, Gordon said he had enjoyed the sand races, and that it had been a "grand week."

Following the sand race was a handicap race for sidecars, with Kristine Rhodes and Brian Davies competing in the injured Geoff Burnhill's outfit. *Scooter World* described the races as "thrilling to watch," but questioned why the results did not count toward the Premier Award.

R E Miles on the mountain section of the full day trial. (MNH)

Premier Award winner Neville Frost – a 27-year-old computer programmer from London, had double reason to celebrate when his wife, Beverley, was crowned Scooter Queen. Neville achieved a record in dropping only 40 points, and also made up part of the winning team 'Ecurie Bromley,' along with championship runner-up Andy Smith, and George Pearce, who finished fifth overall. The Loving Cup Trophy was awarded to Brian and Valerie Morgan, and 19-year-old Linda Watson was declared Scooter Girl.

Rally officials claimed that 1970 was the "highest standard of riding we have ever had," adding that achievements in the 260-mile reliability test had been "remarkable." It was claimed that the biggest test was over the Cringle Reservoir road, and the one-and-a-half mile road known as the 'Whiskey Run.' Despite many riders being unfamiliar with this latest challenge, very few machines got into trouble.[73]

Scooter Girl winner, Linda Watson. (MNH)

Above: Loving Cup winners, Brian and Valerie Morgan. (MNH)

Right: Revellers at the end-of-rally party. (MNH)

For a full listing & details of all our titles please visit – www.veloce.com
All current books • New book news • Special offers • Gift vouchers • Forum

Chapter 15

1971: PORT SODERICK HILL CLIMB

Bill Quayle, chairman of the Tourist Board, was guest of honour at the annual dinner of the Isle of Man Scooter Association, held at the Queen's Hotel on February 12, 1971. Declaring 'Scooter Week' to be "the most important cog in the mosaic of Manx tourism," he promised "every possible support for 1971." Members of the Association were told that the Tourist Board, on which Scooter Week depended for funding, closely followed the event's progress via regular reports received from councillor Charles Burke MHK, who also sat on the committee of the association. Also present was John Ronald from the Lambretta Club of Great Britain, who was twice overall winner of the rally. He predicted that 400 Lambretta riders alone would be travelling to the island in June, resulting in a substantial rise in numbers for the forthcoming event. It was announced that Peter Agg of Lambretta Concessionaires would personally present a prize of £50 to the overall winner, which could be upgraded to £80 if put toward the cost of a new Lambretta GT. J C Bregazzi, chairman of the Isle of Man Scooter Association, thanked the committee for its enthusiasm, especially new secretary Mrs Creer, and clerk to the course Kenny Radcliffe. He predicted a bumper year for 1971.[74]

The programme for Scooter Week was covered in the February issue of *Scooter World*, with congratulations bestowed on the organisers for their idea of charging one fee to cover all activities in 1970, which would also be adopted for 1971.

After the usual get-together on Saturday night at the Falcon Cliff Hotel, Sunday's full day on the TT course was to be followed by the navigational trial in the evening. A meal was provided for competitors between these events, without an increase in the entry fee, and minor changes included a reduction from seven to five in the number of laps, and a half-hour increase in the break before the start of the night trial. A 'Novelty Night' was planned for Monday, and the hill climb event on Tuesday would be followed by a 'Lambretta party' in the evening. A treasure hunt was scheduled for Wednesday evening, along with the Isle of Man Scooter Club's party. The Overall Awards (including the Master Scooterist Badges) would be made on the basis of the Manx full day trial, the hill climb, and the Druidale event, due to take place on the Thursday, and considered to be the climax of the week, as far as the championships were concerned. Sidecars were eligible for all events for the first time, and also the Overall Awards. Due to unfavourable tides, the sand races were scrapped, as they would need to start at 6am, or just before the prize giving ceremony, but a scramble and trial event was to be staged instead.

Scooter World reported that the 1971 Isle of Man Scooter Holiday Week (to give the event its latest official title) would be remembered for its mixed weather, the open nature of the championship, keen competition, the revival of island spirit, and the sporting nature in which it was held. Competitors numbered 100, with over 115 social members, being a few down on the previous year. Despite warnings in the regulations, nine riders arrived without insurance certificates stating that they were covered to take part, although, fortunately, cover was arranged in time for them to compete in the rally.

The rain that had accompanied scooterists on their journey to the island gave way to sunshine by the first day of competition on Sunday morning, when most of the competitors assembled at the grandstand for the start of the full day trial. At 9am, Jim Chappell of Bristol and H A Dudley of Luton were flagged off for the first of five laps on the TT course. Mr Dudley, having completed his first lap, explained that visibility on the mountain was down to 25 yards due to thick fog. The first retirement came at 10.30am, when B Truswell's Heinkel dropped a valve, making a hole in the piston. Upon completion of the five laps, a meal was served in Douglas before the first riders were flagged for the second part of the event: the semi-

Riders prepare for the hill climb. (IOMSC)

treasure hunt taking place in the evening. A train was chartered and filled with over 300 scooterists bound for Castletown, stopping at each station on the way, where questions were answered on sheets provided by the organisers, and handed in at the pub on arrival. The train returned to Douglas after closing time, ending the social highlight of the week.

Tuesday's event at Port Soderick took place on a closed road which included a sharp downhill section, with a sharp left-hand bend about 150 metres from the finish. The length of the course totalled 940 yards (859.5m), with the difference in altitude between start and finish amounting to 237 feet (72.3m). Competitors were dispatched at 30-second intervals, with Ron Moss putting in the best time of 45.4 seconds, a second faster than Paul Gilbert, both riding in the 200cc class. Riders made a total of four runs, with 43.6 seconds Ron Moss' best time, making him 'King of the Hill.' John Foster finished second overall, with Paul Gilbert and W Brunning coming in joint third. The fastest girls were Anne Weir and June Stirrup, both from Manchester, recording times of 58.4 seconds.

A prize giving party for the trial and hill climb events was organised in Port Soderick, with coach transport provided to and from Douglas. The evening was described as: "the only damp squib of the week" by a *Scooter World* correspondent, because the bar manager – deciding that the revellers were too noisy – brought the evening to an early end. Despite this, everyone drank up and left without further prompting.

Another treasure hunt was held on Wednesday – the only event of the day – providing competitors with the opportunity for a well-earned rest, as well as time to prepare for Thursday's Druidale decider. This time, the treasure hunt involved entrants riding their scooters to various points on the island, and it was won by Peter Hasler.

Despite the weather being good in Douglas on Thursday morning, it was already raining in Druidale, scene of the deciding competition for those in contention. The first pair was flagged away at 10.00am, via the open roads to Ballaugh Glen to the time control at the start of the closed section, with the rain now lashing down on the moor. Riding styles differed greatly, with Brian Hull, John Foster and Ron Moss taking the water-splash at speed, and Dave Glover from Yeovil virtually coming to a stop as he went through. Ron Moss claimed an early lead before his carburettor took in water, allowing Brian Hull to overtake, and with John Foster also in contention the riders had to navigate their way through the smaller machines. Toward the end of the final lap, Moss closed the gap to 50 yards on the hill section, but could not catch

sporting trial over a 90 mile (144.8km) route, covering both roads and tracks, and described as "from easy to diabolical." Some competitors opted to take a navigator, but the terrain reduced average speed to around 20mph (32kph).

A popular viewing point was at a ford at Spooyt Vane, at the bottom of a steep, muddy hill. Mr Dudley was de-seated upon hitting the ford, but was later able to re-start after being helped out of the water. Other riders also succumbed – some in the water; some in the mud – having approached the ford too fast. Further difficulties were encountered down a steep, narrow track of grass and loose shale, intersected by the railway tracks halfway down. The route finally ended at Groudle, next to a pub, allowing the competitors to quench their thirst before returning to Douglas, 27 of them achieving gold awards. Outright winner was Ted Parrot with a loss of only nine points for the whole day. Best lady in the event was Moira Roper from Glasgow.

Monday was set aside for rest and repairs, with the

Ian Haynes (75) and George Pearce (97) flat out at Druidale. (MNH)

Brian Hull, known as 'The White Tornado,' by the finish line. The sidecar outfits came next, with Jenny Stevens reportedly nearly drowning her passenger as she came through the water-splash. The junior event was flagged when A Turner from Bridport crashed 100 yards from the finish, and was taken to hospital, after a good-spirited competitor gave up his own chance to help. Alan Mills was the clear winner of the junior event with a loss of 53 points.

The final day's events took place at Knock Froy, over a section of the scramble course. In a day of fierce competition with Gordon Roper from Glasgow coming out on top over Dave Oldland from Bristol in the 104cc class, Andy Mills won the up to 154cc class, and Brian Hull triumphant in the over 154cc class. An all-comers race was also staged, with the small-frame Vespas of Gordon Roper and Dave Oldland performing well against the Lambrettas of George Pearce from Bromley, and Andy Smith, George eventually coming in first.

At the close of Scooter Week, Bill Quayle, chairman of the Isle of Man Tourist Board, presented 22 major prizes at the Majestic Hotel on Friday evening. Manxman Leslie Moore of Douglas (passenger) and Jenny Stevens (Maico) won the Watsonian Challenge Cup for Best Sidecar for the second year running, and Jenny's husband, Malcolm, was presented with the Maico Challenge Cup. For the first time ever the Lady Champion's award was shared, between Anne Lewis (Lambretta) from Luton, and Mrs Stevens.

Ecurie Bromley II won the team prize, and the newcomer's award was claimed by Nigel Burgess (Lambretta) of Peterborough. Winner of the Tynwald Trophy and overall winner was Brian Hull (Lambretta). Clerk to the course Kenny Radcliffe completed the announcements by calling for his wife to receive the Loving Cup for putting up with his long absences during organisation of the event.[75]

Kenny also drew attention to the increasing danger of the Druidale course. "I would like to see it kept but altered to suit rising speeds." He suggested that competitors should start at half-minute intervals, and that a red flag should be used in the event of an accident, allowing the ambulance access straight up the course. He concluded by revealing that the committee was giving serious consideration to a "speed event on closed roads" as part of the following year's programme.[76]

Scooter World ran an editorial in its August issue, lamenting the state of two-wheeled sport on the island in 1971; highlighting Agostini's retirement from the TT races amidst his claim that the course was "no longer safe, and unfit for racing." It was also reported that cycling's professional road race was cancelled due to lack of entries. The 1971 Manx Scooter Week was described as "average," although the magazine was encouraged by the planned introduction of a speed event in 1972, and Kenny Radcliffe's proposed alteration to Druidale. Scooterists were urged to bolster the image of scootering and increase the number of entries for the coming year.

Above: Nigel Burgess, winner of the 1971 Newcomer's Award. (MNH)

Left: Rider 405, Peter Cain in action. (MNH)

Chapter 16

1972: THE FAST MEN OF BALLAUGH

Scooter World correspondent Dave Smith reported that the previous year's rally had been a great week, with the change of pattern generally approved, and backed up by an increase in competitor numbers. The promised speed event led to the introduction of closed road racing on a new circuit near Ballaugh, comprising 2.70 miles (4.35km) in length, and a revised Druidale event run as a hill climb over 4.8 miles (7.72km) of closed road. Grass track racing was introduced, and the full day trial was re-introduced using tracks, with a separate event for the TT course trial.

An early sailing from Liverpool on Saturday, June 17 meant that residents in Douglas were awoken at 4.30am by the exhaust noise of disembarking scooters, with 123 signing up for competitions, and another 160 registering as social members only. Rough seas and disruption at the airport gave way to much improved weather, and the welcoming party was again held at Douglas Head.

Fog persisted until Sunday morning, as the trial got under way from the grandstand at 9.00am. Riders were flagged away by Jim Cain, with 173 miles (278.4km) of tough riding ahead of them. Route cards were not needed in the morning section as the course was signposted, although many of these had been damaged by storms the previous night, causing a problem for two pairs of rally officials who had to replace them, leaving at seven o'clock in the morning. The first section followed a route of mixed mud and stone track, containing one of four ford crossings; this one with a loose gravel base. Riders headed duly south, with the third checkpoint stationed at the southernmost part of the Island. Alan Hillman was an early retirement when he came off and damaged his machine. The course then turned north, weaving its way to the lunch stop at Glen Helen, the 'Whisky Run' section of the course providing its usual excitement, with spectators entertained by "some quite spectacular manoeuvres and falls."

After a one-and-a-half hour break and a number of repairs, surviving riders embarked on the next section, with another ford to be navigated after two miles (3.2km). Having a concrete base, riders were able to approach the ford at speed, much to the cost of spectators standing nearby. The route then followed north before veering east and through Sulby ford, on to Ramsey, and then southward through Laxey, and the lanes to Glen Roy: the venue of a 'Special Stage' consisting of a steep climb over 1¼ miles, starting on large rocks that thinned out to grass and mud before turning to gravel. The course continued to Windy Corner up the side of a hill, with a small stream running down its surface. Many riders failed to negotiate the fast mud section, but an easier section now led to the finish at Groudle Glen.

The results were announced the following morning, when it was declared that although 66 of the 82 starters completed the course, only 20 of them received gold awards, with 31 silver and 12 bronze. With the loss of just three points, Luke Kitto was declared the full day trial winner. This event was a major success for the Vespa camp, which claimed six out of the first seven places, and nine in the first 13.

The good weather held out for the next day, with riders heading up to Ballaugh for a practice round of the race circuit, some blissfully unaware that the road was still open, resulting in a few near misses. Scrutineering went on throughout the afternoon, with official practice sessions beginning at 6.00pm, coinciding with a break in the weather and the arrival of rain, which persisted for the duration of the event.

Arthur Quinney flagged off the first race at 7.00pm – a mixed event for 150cc standard and 200ccc special classes, which soon separated out on the track – with Ian Hemming winning the first race in the 150cc class, and Ray Kemp in the 200cc. The second race was a sidecar event, with only five of the ten entries starting: retirements were one non-starter for the practice; two crashes in practice; one refusing to start due to the weather, and an engine problem with the remaining machine. Alan Burton raced to an early lead in his specially-constructed, right-hand outfit, and, despite a strong challenge from Tony Walsh, held out for a winning margin of 0.4 seconds.

The third race was a mixed class event, with victories for John Ronald, Andy Smith, Ray Kemp, and George Pearce, and finally, the last race was an invitational event for all classes of machine, and both solo riders and team entries. Ray Kemp suffered a 30-second delay when his machine failed to start, but by lap two had whittled away Alan Flack's lead at the rate of eight seconds per lap. By the fourth lap – and just three seconds behind – he had made a successful assault on the lead position, recording an actual average of 58mph (93.34kph). The roads re-opened at 9.30pm, and scooterists made for the Jurby Hotel for a party which went on until 1.00am.

Noon the following day saw the start of the TT course trial, consisting of five laps to be completed at an average speed of 30mph (48.28kph). There were 86 starters, with 22 dropping out by the finish. The riders in contention for awards largely completed the course without accruing penalty points, but George Pearce and Anne Weir were forced to retire with mechanical problems. The weather was good for the most part, with some of the riders experiencing rain on the mountain in the latter stages.

Scrutineering for the Druidale event took place at the Ballaugh end of the course on Thursday morning, run as a hill climb over the closed section of road. Competitors were vying for a starting position to avoid being held back by slower machines, and although there was a brief downpour at noon, the sunshine returned to provide unusually good weather for this event. This year, only the fastest run for each rider was to count, encouraging entrants to put in a good first lap, in case they should experience problems at a later stage. Last year's winner, Brian Hull, made a good start, but the race was stopped when Andy Chadd hit a cattle grid at speed and went into a bank. Taken to Ramsey by ambulance, he suffered only relatively minor injuries.

Following the re-start, there were a number of forced retirements, including Haydn Redfern (engine mounting); Pete Woodland and Dave Oldland (engine seizure). The

second lap was completed without incident, although a sidecar outfit hit a wall on the third lap, fortunately without injury to the occupants, and the bike of a solo rider had the panels ripped off as he hit the water, the marshals quickly removing these to prevent them unseating the rider following. A fourth run was completed by some of the riders, with the road closure order bringing the event to an end at 4pm. Results were withheld until Friday, to keep the name of the overall winner under wraps until the presentation ceremony, but Alan Flack recoded the fastest run of 6 minutes 12 seconds, returning an average speed of 46.4mph (74.67kph), with Queen of the Hill June Stirrup completing the course in 7 minutes 42.2 seconds.

The fourth round of the Grass Track Championship – jointly hosted by the Lambretta Club of Great Britain and the IOM Scooter Association – was held on Friday. Located behind the grandstand, the course provided a good day's racing enjoyed by all present, with the weather holding out, despite blustery and cloudy conditions. Newcomer Kevin Walkman was placed in all five solo classes, with three firsts, one second, and one third, and won what was described as both of the 'Devil take the hindmost' events.

Next was the prize presentation at the Majestic Hotel, with the awards made by Mr J C Bregazzi, chairman of the IOMSA. The first awards presented were the Master Scooterists Shields and Year Bars, presented to all who completed the three championship events without any fails. Next up were the TT trial, grass track and Druidale, and, amidst much tension, Andy Smith (Lambretta) was called forward as overall winner on 104 points, ahead of Luke Kitto, second with 113 points, and the full day trial winner, and fastest over the special stages. Scooter Queen was Anne Lewis, (Lambretta), ranked 15th overall, and the sidecar award went to Doug Mansfield and Paul Amos. The team award was claimed by the Vespa-riding trio nicknamed 'The Councillors,' consisting of Luke Kitto, Ted Parrot, and Steven Roberts. The newcomer award was presented to Steven Roberts (Vespa).

80 advance entries were taken for the 1973 rally, and Druidale was declared the best attended event of 1972 with 107 entries.

Chapter 17

1973: DRUIDALE RECORD SMASHED

Dates for the 1973 rally – now a real speed event with results contributing to national championships – were announced as June 16-23. The full day trial was to count toward the FoBSC (Federation of British Scooter Clubs) Trial Championship; road racing at Ballaugh was to count toward the FoBSC British Scooter Track Championship, and the grass track racing toward the FoBSC Grass Track Championship.[77]

Following Saturday night's get-together, hosted by compère Roy Bocock and master of ceremonies Dave Smith, Sunday played host to the all-day trial. The event finished at Douglas Head, where competitors had to negotiate six different sections without putting a foot on the ground, resulting in a tie between Nick Banks (Vespa) and D Brown (Lambretta combination).

Rider 329 negotiates Braddan Bridge. (MNH)

J C Bregazzi wields the starter's flag. (MNH)

Rider 352, Luke Kitto. (MNH)

On Monday evening, riders competed in one of two road race meetings at Ballaugh, but disaster struck when three riders – Peter Chapman, John Ronald, and Ray Smith – collided in a high-speed incident, all requiring treatment at Ramsey Cottage Hospital. Fortunately, the three made a speedy recovery.

Ballaugh race circuit played host to the 4th round of the British Road Race Championship on Wednesday, with records broken in every class. Doug May recorded a lap speed of 61.98mph (99.74kph), and the sidecar outfit of Neville Frost and wife Beverley set the combination record of 53.96mph (86.84kph). Winner of the main race was Ray Kemp, whose gearbox broke up at the finishing line.[78]

Neville Frost reported in *Club and Circuit Magazine* that riders in 1973 were successfully forced by the FoBSC to ride in the Isle of Man, and to compete in two events, in order to qualify for the FoBSC Road Race Championship: Neville chose to ride in the Ballaugh Road Race and at

George Pearce (54) and Mick Jones (44) preparing to leave the grandstand. (MNH)

Druidale in both the combination and solo classes, having won the solo event in 1969 and 1970.

Upon inspection, it was found that the base of the ford at Druidale no longer comprised several slabs with gaps in-between, but was a solid piece of concrete covered by an inch of water. This meant that although the water-splash would still look spectacular when taken at speed, there was far less danger of riders coming off.

Good weather conditions prevailed, and, despite losing a panel from the Paul Marshall Comerfords-sponsored 200, Nev smashed the six minute barrier by almost 11 seconds, and recorded a time of 6 minutes and 42 seconds in the combo with passenger, Bev (despite the carburettor taking in water at the splash): a time bettered by just eight solo machines. The solo machine started well but then disaster struck when the Lambretta broke its piston rings, and, due to lack of spares, had to be rebuilt with only the bottom ring intact. Despite the handicap, the 200 was clocked at 70.60mph (113.61kph) on the final lap.

The last competition held was Friday's grass track race meeting, at which Alan Kean won the 125, 150, and 200 classes. However, *Jet Set* reported that, in the 200 class, Alan mistakenly thought the last lap flag was the chequered flag, and pulled into the paddock, not realizing his mistake until it was too late. Readers of *Classic Scooterist Scene* will be aware of the controversy surrounding the 1973 rally, as reported by Geoff Stephens, of the Hampshire Wildcats SC 'Wildcat' works team. Geoff rode a Lambretta 150, with all the special classification machines up to 225cc taking part, distinguished by different coloured race numbers. Ray Kemp and Doug May came in first, followed by Geoff on the smaller machine (although he was first in the 150cc class). Geoff stated he had mistakenly been awarded the third place trophy in the 225cc class, and passed it on to Dick Wolfgang, the rightful recipient. The first place trophy in the 150cc class – and new class lap record – was awarded to Nigel Burgess, who finished some distance behind Geoff in fourth place overall. Despite Geoff's protests, the official records were never amended.[79]

1973 Overall Champion was Andy Smith (Lambretta) for the second year running, and Lady Champion was Liz Chappell (Vespa). Dave Brown (Lambretta) was Sidecar Champion, with J Davison (Vespa) claiming the newcomer's award. Nick Banks was declared winner of the full day trial.

For a full listing & details of all our titles please visit – www.veloce.com
All current books • New book news • Special offers • Gift vouchers • Forum

113

Chapter 18

1974: BRING ON THE BIKES

The 17th Isle of Man Rally was scheduled to take place between June 15 and 21, 1974, and would, for the first time, allow lightweight motorcycles up to 175cc, and class 8 machines up to 104cc, with class 9 relating to motorcycles from 104 to 175cc. The weekend began with registration and scrutineering, followed by an informal gathering at the Villiers Hotel on Douglas promenade, described by *Scooter and Scooterist* in its June issue as a "grand evening" with disco and games, the drink "fast-flowing," and the Scotland team victorious in the 'World Cup Balloons' event. At the end of the evening, Ken Radcliffe delivered a pep talk on the full day trial, and a *Scooter and Scooterist* correspondent reported that the previous year's rally was "taken apart" for its slackness and slow full day trial, and having the Druidale event as the rally decider. Because of this, only four gold awards were presented for the 250 mile (402km) event. Competitors had to check in bang on the second with a minute's allowance to gain the top award, and there were synchronized chronometers at each checkpoint.

Ideal weather prevailed for the 1974 Scooter Week, and the full day trial was flagged off from Douglas at 8.30am, passing through Peel, Castletown, Port St Mary, and duly north to Druidale, Jurby and Sulby for a half-hour break. From Sulby, the route progressed to Laxey, Onchan, back to Druidale, Peel, and on to Douglas via the back woods, taking in the 'Whiskey Run' and 'Horsepack Gully.'

The previous year's winner, Nick Banks, competed in a sidecar outfit with Andrew Spencer, and the sidecars were first away, followed by Colin Hart, first solo rider, ten minutes later. Norrie Kerr had suffered a puncture by the first checkpoint, and later seized his engine trying to make up lost time. George Pierce was upended on the grassy tracks and suffered a broken collarbone: a sad end to his competitive week. Steve Roberts was also delayed by a puncture, and broke a gear cable coming to the aid of

Liz Chappell. Despite picking up a second puncture on the run-in, he did manage to finish, however. Colin Hart was forced into an exhaust change when his original pipe cracked and broke around the Druidale section of the course.

In total, ten motorcycles took part, with J Howie the best placed. Jenny Stevens was declared Best Lady, just missing out on a gold award with her sidecar partner, Les Moore. 1st-4th positions, and winners of the gold awards, were Luke Kitto, Ted Parrot, Andy Smith, and Dave Oldland.

The event was hailed as the best trial held on the island for the last three years, possibly longer, and the difficult nature of the event made it worthy of a road trial championship. Clerk of the course Ken Radcliffe and his assistant, Ken Bridson, were awarded full marks by *Scooter and Scooterist* for their organisation of the event.[80]

Next in the proceedings was Tuesday's TT regularity test, run in breezy but otherwise perfect weather conditions. The first rider was flagged off at 11.00am on a route which consisted of five laps of the TT course, giving a grand total of 190 miles (305.8km). The road was not closed for this event, which passed without major incident, setting the stage for Druidale, which, this year, did not have the deciding influence of previous years, although a good result would enable riders to improve their overall position. Tuesday's dance and presentation followed the regularity test, with Villiers again hosting the party, which went on until midnight on this occasion; once the medals had been given out for the full day trial and the regularity test, revellers returned to the serious business of the evening: drinking.

Scooter and Scooterist correspondent Colin Hart reported on the Jurby races, which took place between June 17 and 19, and was his first time at the IOM rally. Despite the friendly and sociable atmosphere, Colin

Awards presentation event of 1974. (MNH)

1 Keith Shaw 2 Steve Hanlon 3 Dave Oldland
4 George Pearce 5 Steve Roberts 6 Duncan McKenzie
7 John Ronald 8 Liz Chappel 9 Gerry Murphy 10 Luke
Kitto 11 Duncan Findlayson 12 Ted Parrot 13 Andy
Smith 14 Colin Hart 15 Brian Morgan 16 Norrie Kerr

learned that a rift now existed between the racing and rallying camps, and commented that turnout for the Jurby races was "pathetic." He pointed out that the full day trial was more likely to cause damage to a machine than racing would, and questioned why more competitors were not prepared to participate in the speed events. He did, however, concede that "the track had the bumpiest surface graced by the name of tarmacadam to feature in the Isle of Man races." Speaking in 2014, Manx competitor Les Moore explained to the author that local riders entered the rally on the machines they used for work, and could not compete against tuned machines, brought to the

island especially to race. Seven riders took part in the first race, which was won by Colin Hart, with Norrie Kerr coming a close second. Only three riders began the class two race, and with Dave Webster dropping out, it was left to Vic Dachtler and Ann Weir to finish the race.

The remaining races were run in groups, due to the small number of competitors, but because of loose gravel on the track, riders were 'shot-blasted' along the start and finish straight by the rider in front. The 150 class was convincingly won by Steve Ives, who almost lapped the second-placed finisher. Class four was the largest entry with nine finishers, and although Ray Kemp was expected to do well, first place went to Doug May, followed by Mick Hayman. The 150 specials class was won by Tony Moss, and Ray Kemp was a convincing winner in the big specials class. Manx competitor Jenny Stevens took an early lead in the combination class, and, despite being caught by Dave Dalton, managed to remain in front. The condition of the track led to all but one of the combination fairings becoming detached. Colin also made special mention of Bill Metcalf, who managed to claim three of the 40 gallon drums on one lap, fortunately, at the relatively small cost of a dented leg shield.

Glorious weather prevailed for Thursday's Druidale circuit, now a closed road event of approximately 4.75 miles (7.64km) of single track road with a steep hill at the start, dropping down to the water-splash. *Scooter and Scooterist* reported that the road was also home to cattle grids, hairpins and gravel, but described Druidale as "the best scooter hill climb in the world." This was the first time that Druidale did not act as the rally decider, although it would be remembered for the record being twice smashed by Ray Kemp: riding an Arthur Francis 200, he broke Nev Frost's record by an incredible four seconds to win the 200cc specials class.

Andy Smith prevailed in the 125 class, with Luke Kitto taking second place. Steve Ellis triumphed in the 200 class, and Norrie Kerr edged in front of Dave Oldland to take the 90cc class. There were two classes for the sidecar event, with D Brown and R Bull winning on the upright machines, despite a strong challenge from Jenny Stevens and Pete Murray. Comfortable winners of the racing sidecars were Lincon riders Dave Dalton and Judy Jubb. The motorcycle classes were won by D Butler (Suzuki 100), and G Wendt (Suzuki 125).[81]

Thursday evening hosted a trip on the railway to Castletown, during a night that was not without controversy, with a streak by Jim Neil of Birmingham, and high spirits on the return trip resulting in the train being stopped to prevent passengers disembarking from a moving carriage. Unfortunately, a carriage window was broken, incurring a repair bill for the IOMSA. Highlight of the social week was Friday's presentation, prize giving, and cabaret, at which Ken Radcliffe was presented with a silver salver from competitors for his work as clerk to the course over the last ten years. The cabaret included a stripper, who discovered a most able assistant in Malcolm Black ...

First overall, and winner of the Tynwald Trophy and £25 (plus an extra £10 put up by *Scooter and Scooterist*) was Andy Smith (Lambretta). The Deuxieme and Troisieme awards were won by Luke Kitto and Dave Oldland respectively. Scooter Queen and winner of the Liz Smolen trophy was Mrs Liz Chappell (Vespa), which earnt her a £10 prize, the same going to the winner of Best Sidecar and the Watsonian Trophy, Jenny Stevens (Maico). Torbay Scooter Club won the Team Prize, and G Wendt from New Zealand won the premier motorcycle award: the Villiers Trophy.

Other awards included Best Maico Driver (Jenny Stevens); Vespa Challenge Cup (Luke Kitto); Wallace Challenge Cup (Malcolm Black); the ScotManx Trophy (Norrie Kerr); the LCGB Cup (Andy Smith); BLOA Rose Bowl (S Ives), and the Vespa Newcomer's Trophy (Colin Hart). Following the presentations, Ken Radcliffe urged competitors to return for the following year's competition, with over one hundred of them answering his call.

For a full listing & details of all our titles please visit – www.veloce.com
All current books • New book news • Special offers • Gift vouchers • Forum

Chapter 19

1975: SEPTEMBER RALLY

For 1975, the rally was finally moved to September 6-13, after the Manx Grand Prix, as had been suggested many years before, and was now marketed as the Isle of Man Motor Cycle and Scooter Rally. The first day of competition was to be a 200 mile (321.9km) green lane trial on Sunday, followed by all-day racing at Jurby, counting toward the Track Championship (scooters only). Tholt-y-Will was the venue for Tuesday's hill climb event, with a night road trial that evening. The TT course trial was scheduled for Wednesday, with Druidale in its regular slot on Thursday. Friday was to host the giant slalom event at Noble's Park, followed by a night out in Ramsey. A week-long treasure hunt was also organised, taking competitors all over the island, and offering substantial prizes in order to give wives, children, and those visiting solely for the social events plenty to do throughout the week. The Overall and Premier Awards were to be judged on the full day trial, hill climb (best run to count), night road trial, TT course trial, and Druidale (also on best run).

Upon arrival to the Island, the usual scrutineering took place at the grandstand between 10am and 8pm, under the charge of Jeff Rolfe. The Villiers was once again chosen as the venue for the welcoming party, where Ken Radcliffe greeted the competitors, and gave them their instructions for the week ahead.

The following morning, Bob Young was the first man away at 9am, followed by around 150 riders at one-minute intervals. The enduro trial was a navigational exercise, run at a constant average speed of 25mph (40.23kph), with checkpoints at previously undisclosed sites, where riders' times of passing were checked by chronometers accurate to one second. Scooter and Scooterist reported that the official timekeepers were slightly out, and credit went to IOM Association secretary Dave Higgins for rectifying the situation. During the enduro some riders took a wrong turn, including Norrie Kerr, although he recovered in time to claim a silver award; just missing out on the

gold. Despite carburettor trouble (as in bits falling off), Liz Chappell finished strongly, but Keith Cowans was not so lucky, retiring with a stripped flywheel. Sheila Thomas also retired after breaking a clutch cable. John Davidson emerged victorious on his 250cc Suzuki, in front of Andy Smith on his Lambretta Combo. Luke Kitto (Vespa) took third place.[82] Team Nickspeed reported it had stashed gallon cans of petrol at friendly petrol stations, their sidecar outfit – nicknamed the 'Hairy Chair' – returning 30-40 miles per gallon.

Monday's Jurby races were held in similar conditions to the previous year: competitors expressed displeasure about the mass of loose chippings, but were advised by Scooter and Scooterist to be grateful to the IOMSA for providing racing events, urging people to come forward with suggestions for improvement rather than criticism. The races were divided into eight classes, with Ian and Terry Frankland, Dave Webster, and D Wolfang all achieving class wins. Jenny Stevens and R Myres triumphed in class 7 (sidecars); M Hayman (Lambretta) took first place in the Manx invitational race (solo), with Don Browning and Kevin Barns winning the combo event, also on a Lambretta.

Tuesday's Tholt-y-Will hill climb was a new event, and well received, despite the bleak weather and light rain. The course also hosted car racing in the form of the RAC hill climb, which carried international status. The motorcycles, with their extra power, were better equipped for the hill climb, Bob Young, for one, unhappy with his Vespa 125 machine, which was slower than some of the 90cc machines, and Colin Prior lost a set of engine lugs on his Lambretta whilst negotiating the climb. There were ten classes in total (1-9 with two categories within class 7 sidecars), with the winners listed in order: Ian Frankland (Vespa); John Ronald (Lambretta); Dave Webster (Lambretta); M Hayman (Lambretta); Dave Webster (Lambretta); Ray Kemp

(Lambretta); Don Browning/K Barnes (Lambretta); C Fergusson/J Kershaw (Lambretta); P Allen (Suzuki), and lastly J W Williams (CZ).

Jenny Stevens was first rider away on Tuesday evening's night trial, followed by Norrie Kerr on the first solo machine. The trial was again timed by the watches of marshals, with no errors on this occasion. The course headed south to Ballasalla, Castletown, and back to Douglas via more inland routes. Andy Smith lost a silencer halfway around the course, considerably reducing the power of his combo machine, though he strenuously denied that he made Pauline push on some of the tough sections! Some riders finished the event without lights, and, according to *Scooter and Scooterist*, Norrie Kerr finished with Colin Hart's clutch lever (readers were invited to figure out for themselves how this happened!), and Norrie and Colin finished in 7th and 5th places respectively.

John Davidson, winner of the full day trial, was unseated, twisting his handlebars and breaking a gear change lever in the process. Despite this, he managed to complete the course in 18th place. Luke Kitto emerged victorious in first place, making it a one-two for Vespa, with S Hanlon coming in second.

Wednesday's regularity trial was the only day of competition for some riders, including Isobel Thompson who claimed her second bronze award. Unfortunately, Dave Webster's wife, Lyn, was not so fortunate, racking up a grand total of 14,515 penalty points! In the evening, competitors returned to the Villiers for the full day trial awards, and Avon Valley's presentation of 'Cavalcade of Speed' awards. The evening ended early, with many of the competitors contemplating the Druidale event the following morning.

One Druidale competitor – Alan Foxton – was lucky to escape serious injury on his second run, as he approached the summit during a downpour. Opting to corner on a cattle grid, the slippery conditions caused him to be thrown from his machine, and he ended up on the other side of the wall. Despite extensive damage to his machine, an x-ray revealed that a suspected broken leg was only heavy bruising.

Ian and Terry Frankland triumphed in classes 1 and 2 respectively, riding Taffspeed Lambrettas, and Dave Webster returned a time of 58.6 seconds in the 150 class, beating the time of class 4 winner Steve Ellis on a 200cc machine. Winners of the remaining classes were Dave Webster (Lambretta); Ray Kemp (Lambretta); Don Browning/Kevin Barnes (Lambretta); Andy and Pauline Smith (Lambretta); P Allen (Suzuki), and Neil Buttery, (Ossa). Ray Kemp set a new record of 5.22.2 seconds, and Don Browning and Kevin Barnes beat Neville Frost's combination record. *Scooter and Scooterist* reported that Thursday's entertainment, billed as a 'Novelty Night Out at Ramsey Regatta,' had been cancelled due to the weather, leaving a choice of striptease at the Falcon Cliff Hotel, or Norrie Kerr buying a round of drinks at the Quarterbridge![83]

Andy and Pauline Smith were the best combo riders in Friday's slalom event, held on grass and tarmacadam, and fortunately walked away unhurt after rolling their Lambretta outfit. Best solo rider was Neil Buttery, and the best lady was Ann Weir. The presentation evening was again held at the Majestic, where it was announced that Kenny Radcliffe would be retiring after the following year's event.

The First Overall Tynwald Trophy was awarded jointly to Andy and Pauline Smith (Lambretta), together with £25 in prize money, plus £10 from *Scooter and Scooterist*. Andy and Pauline were also presented with the LCGB Cup, the LASCA Award, and Best Sidecar. The Deuxieme Award went to Luke Kitto (Vespa), who also took the Best Vespa Award, and, as a member of Torbay SC, winner of the Team Award. The Troisieme Award was won by Colin Hart. First Motorcycle and Trophy winner was John Whittal Williams. Liz Chappell (Vespa) was crowned Lady Champion for the third successive year, and received The Elizabeth Smolen Trophy, and the ScotManx Trophy winner was John Davidson (Suzuki).

Other winners were T Frazer (Greeves) best British Machine; B Mills (Suzuki) SELSA Award; A Weir (Suzuki) EMSA Award, and J W Williams (CZ) Newcomer's Award. Lastly, Scotland walloped England 5-2 in the football competition. Norrie Kerr managed to get on the score sheet for Scotland, with Ted Parrott and J Neil scoring consolation goals for England.

Chapter 20

1976: END OF THE ROAD

Unbeknown to competitors, the 1976 event – or 'Holiday Week for Motorcyclists and Scooterists,' as it was now promoted – would be their last. Taking place between September 11 and 18, the president of the Isle of Man Scooter Association was Jim Cain, OBE, and the committee at the time of the final rally were as follows: chairman E J Coward; results officer and vice chairman G A Quinney JP; clerk to the course and chief marshal Kenny Radcliffe; deputy clerk to the course C D Bridson; deputy chief marshal D Brookes; route marker A Newton; deputy results officer R Skillicorn; chief scrutineer and secretary Dave Higgins. Chief steward for the event was Dave Smith of the Federation of British Scooter Clubs. The rally programme announced the death of John Chalmers Bregazzi, vice president, and, for eight years, chairman, of the IOMSA.

The first event was Sunday's full day trial, beginning at 9.00am, with H Dudley the first man away on the first of two 100 mile (160.9km) laps to be covered at an average speed of 20mph (32.19kph), the motorcycles clocking up lower mileages and setting a higher average speed. Regular tracks were used, including the Whisky Run, Druidale, and a new track at Narradale. The route map also revealed a bog section, made even more difficult by Saturday's heavy rainfall. The scene was described as "a battlefield, with bikes being manhandled everywhere." Last year's champions, Andy and Pauline Smith, suffered from suspension collapse on their combo, and, despite dropping his Kawasaki and suffering an injured knee, Keith Shaw managed to finish the course. Favourable weather conditions prevailed throughout the event, but the second lap ended the race for local rider Neil Kelly, who broke a leg. Colin Hart put in the best performance on a scooter, and reported that, upon completion of the second lap, riders were sent down a narrow path obscured by bracken and fern, when he was confronted by Mike Webster coming the other way! After a brief face-off, both

riders agreed to continue up the track. Geoff Cannell and Luke Kitto claimed the first two places on motorcycles; Colin Hart came third, and winners of the sidecar award were Jenny Stevens and Les Moore (Maico).

The weather turned for Monday's TT course time trial, with dreadful conditions compounded by shorter lap times over five laps, equating to approximately 190 miles (306km). Of the 41 starters, 29 finished the event, one of whom was Colin Hart, despite seizing his engine on numerous occasions. Luke Kitto managed to lose his time sheet with one-and-a-half laps to go, but Norrie Kerr – who rode with him all night – generously provided him with the times. Keith Shaw, having badly bruised his knee in the previous event, was forced to retire (though, fortunately, recovered sufficiently to referee Friday's football match). Finishing at 2.00am, Dave Jupp and Mike Webster put in the best performances, both acquiring just 50 penalty points each.[84]

The well-received Tholt-y-Will hill climb event was retained for 1976, and was the third to count toward the overall awards. Competitors gathered ready for the 12.00 noon start. Colin Hart, still suffering from engine seizures, discovered the cause after stripping his carburettor, and was soon back in contention. Victory was not to be his, however, as Steve Hare's race-tuned Vespa 100 proved too fast in class 1.

Classes were run in the order 6 to 1, followed by class 7, with the first trips described as "test runs at speed." The course took in two hairpins – left and right – followed by a long incline, a couple of gradual left-hand corners, a 90 degree left on a cattle grid; followed by the last two hairpins, left and right. In class 3, four of Mick Hayman's runs (Lambretta GP 200) were under one minute 50 seconds, making him 'King of the Hill' with a best time of one minute 47.5 seconds. Speaking to *Scooter and Scooterist*, Mick reported that "The course was very demanding, needing not only good riding, but fast

Riders assemble at the Tholt-y-Will Inn in 1976. Back row, L-R: Ted Carter, Jim Neil, Jenny Stevens, Steve Marsay, Malcolm Stevens (bending); front row, L-R: Iggy Prackauskas, Rick Simpson. (MNH)

acceleration, good braking, and a keen eye for any sheep or cattle."

Dave Webster also recorded a very good time of one minute 54 seconds on his GP 150. June Stirrup (Lambretta 150) was 'Queen of the Hill' with her fastest time of two minutes 17.8 seconds. The Suzuki TS 125s were the fastest bikes, leaving Luke Kitto no chance of

a class win on his Honda 150, and Iggy Mycock and passenger Eddie Carter, along with Jenny Stevens and Kenny Radcliffe, won the sidecar classes. John Ronald recorded a creditable lap of one minute 59.8 seconds on his Vespa 125.

A potentially serious accident occurred involving Colin Prior and Martin Bailey when, lying in a strong position, the combo crashed at the 90 degree bend, and was completely written-off. Fortunately, neither rider or passenger suffered serious injury, and were praised by *Scooter and Scooterist* for remaining cheerful, and offering help and encouragement to others, despite the damage to their machine. The event drew to a close at 4pm, hailed a great success.[85]

Good weather remained for Wednesday's 100 mile (160.9km) green lane regularity trial, consisting of five, 20 mile route-marked laps, and leaving the grandstand at 11.00am. There were six checkpoints, and sections of metalled roads which allowed riders to make up lost time and hit the checkpoint bang on time to the second. Keith Shaw came out of retirement with his knee heavily bandaged, and Colin Hart went on to finish 11th, despite dropping his machine. The first three finishers were Dave Minskip, Geoff Cannell, and Luke Kitto, all riding motorcycles. Best placed scooter was that of Liz Chappell, who "did not put a foot wrong." Andy Smith collided with an obstacle, bending his forks and cracking his sidecar frame, yet still managed to finish. The trial ended at 3.30pm, 10 miles (16.1km) south of Douglas, with riders' thoughts now on Thursday's Druidale event.

Druidale was described in *Scooter and Scooterist* as "the best event of its kind," and, despite the fact that motorcycles had also been competing for the last three years, the record was still held by a scooter. The good weather continued, allowing the races to begin on schedule at 11.00am. Terry Frankland entered on his newly-prepared Taffspeed 150 Vespa, and was second fastest in class 2. *Scooter and Scooterist* editor Norrie Kerr pointed out, however, that, despite winning the Vespa Trophy for Best Standard Vespa for the second year running, his machine was, in fact, "more tuned than my bagpipes."[86] Finishing 4th in class 2, Norrie returned a time of six minutes 50.6 seconds on a bog-standard Vespa 125 – faster than several entrants in the 200cc class. Having replaced the road engine he had used all week with his race-tuned unit, Colin Hart won the 100cc class, and Mick Hayman (Lambretta) was the fastest scooter over Druidale.

With the roads re-opening at 4pm, there was time for four circuits, and Dave Webster, despite hitting a wall, managed to win class 2 in six minutes, 0. 5 seconds. Tony Moss dropped his machine at Chevron Corner, cracking a rib in the process, but still returned a fast time of six minutes flat on his only completed run. Andy and Pauline Smith won class 6 on their combo, with Iggy Mycock and Eddie Carter the victors in class 7. Vic Madely (Fantic

125) and Will Priestly (Ossa 250) won their motorcycles' respective classes.

Port Soderick was the venue for Thursday night's disco, where Norrie Kerr celebrated his 30th birthday and was given the bumps, enthusiastically hurled up to the ceiling a number of times. A discounted ferry sailing meant that most competitors left Friday's presentation ceremony at 10.45pm in order to make the sailing, bringing the festivities of the final scooter rally to a premature end.

The final Premier Award and Tynwald Trophy were awarded to Luke Kitto; Best Lady, Best Sidecar and Watsonian Trophy, and the Maico Challenge Cup all went to Jenny Stevens. Colin Hart won the Slazenger Trophy, and Will Priestly won Best Motorcyclist and the Best Newcomer's Trophy. Team Wasps – consisting of Norrie Kerr, Dave Tipping, Steve Hare, and Alan Hodson – claimed the team award; Norrie also won the ScotManx Trophy. Terry Moore added to his large haul of awards with the Wallace Challenge Cup, this time riding a Suzuki. England was denied the opportunity to avenge the previous year's trashing in the football competition, as this year it was to be Vespa against Lambretta, with the Lambretta team victorious by six goals to four.

Although many competitors planned to return in 1977 it was not to be, and, despite a petition being presented to the Isle of Man Tourist Board, it was decided that the event had run its course. *Scooter and Scooterist* magazine sent an open letter to the Board, to which secretary Leonard Bond replied, stating that the petition had been somewhat premature, as a decision would not be made until mid-November, when the 1976 accounts and attendance figures would be put before the race committee. Editor Norrie Kerr hoped that the magazine's actions would help avert cancellation of the event, but Kenny Radcliffe's retirement left only Dave Higgins in the driving seat. Speaking in 2012, Kenny recalled a conversation with Dave, in which they decided to end the event on a high, rather than wait for the Tourist Board to pull the plug on funding, and watch Scooter Week go the same way as Cycling Week.

Throughout the seventies, interest in scooters had been on the decline, and, despite small motorcycles being allowed to compete since 1974, the numbers involved were just no longer viable.

And so ended an island tradition that had endured for twenty years, with the single exception of 1966: it had been a remarkable event, with which many of the organisers had been involved for much of that time, and some even from the very start.

Chapter 21

1980: OUTLAWED

The last competitive Isle of Man Scooter Rally took place just two years before the release of the movie *Quadrophenia*, and the subsequent 'Mod' revival, which developed into a new generation of scooter-riding youths in the early 1980s known as 'Scooter-boys.' Rallies were organised on a huge scale as purely social events, and attended by scooterists at seaside resorts throughout the UK.

From as early as the late 1970s, the Isle of Man government had been concerned about the prospect of trouble that was often reported at these events. Approximately 900 scooterists travelled to the Isle of Man during the 1980 August Bank Holiday, and organiser Alan Eves predicted that they would return in their thousands in 1981. However, they were prevented from doing so, as the Executive Council called an emergency meeting, and imposed a ban on scooters coming to the island: the steam packet and Sealink ordered not to embark any groups of scooters without Manx registrations. Government secretary Peter Hulme stated that Tynwald did not wish to see a repeat of the "serious violence and criminal damage that had occurred elsewhere,"[87] and it was reported that Manx police were carefully monitoring air and sea arrivals against the threat of a Bank Holiday 'invasion.'

On 23 April, 1981, the *Manx Star* headlined on its front page that the Executive Council was considering upholding 1980's decision to keep out "hordes of marauding Mods, involved in street fighting and looting in mainland resorts." Calls for an extended ban were made following reports of further violence during the Easter Bank Holiday, during which, it was claimed, fighting had broken out between gangs of Mods and Skinheads.

The restriction on visiting scooters – in large groups, in any case – continued, and remained in place until 2002. The following year, the Lambretta Club of Great Britain announced the Isle of Man Bank Holiday Weekender, to be held between May 2 and 5, in celebration of the club's first 50 years. Turnout was modest, but the scooters returned to the island in 2003 in their number for an event that included a ride-out on the TT course, a custom show in Peel, and a sprint session at Jurby airfield.

The Isle of Man Scooter Club still thrives today, organising events throughout the year, including gymkhanas, ride-outs, and numerous social gatherings. The Isle of Man Scooter Rally has since been re-instated as a bi-annual social event, still drawing crowds of scooterists of all ages.

More great scooter & motorcycle books from Veloce!

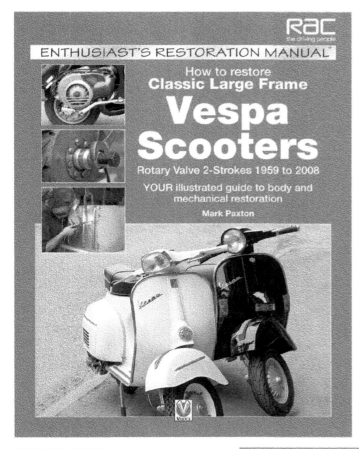

9781787110281

9781787114081

9781845840952

Tel 01305 260068/email: info@veloce.co.uk
for details

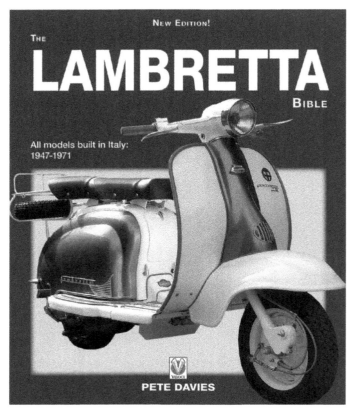

9781787111394

9781845844943

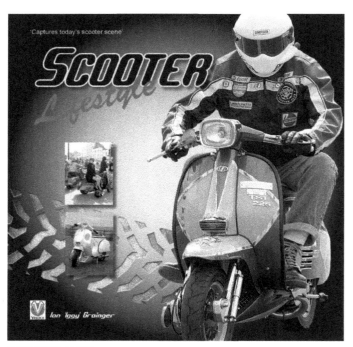

9781787111196

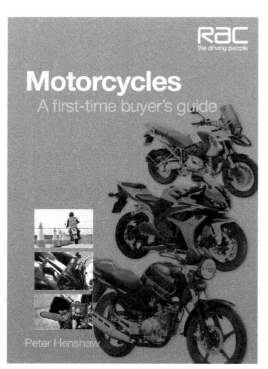

9781845844950

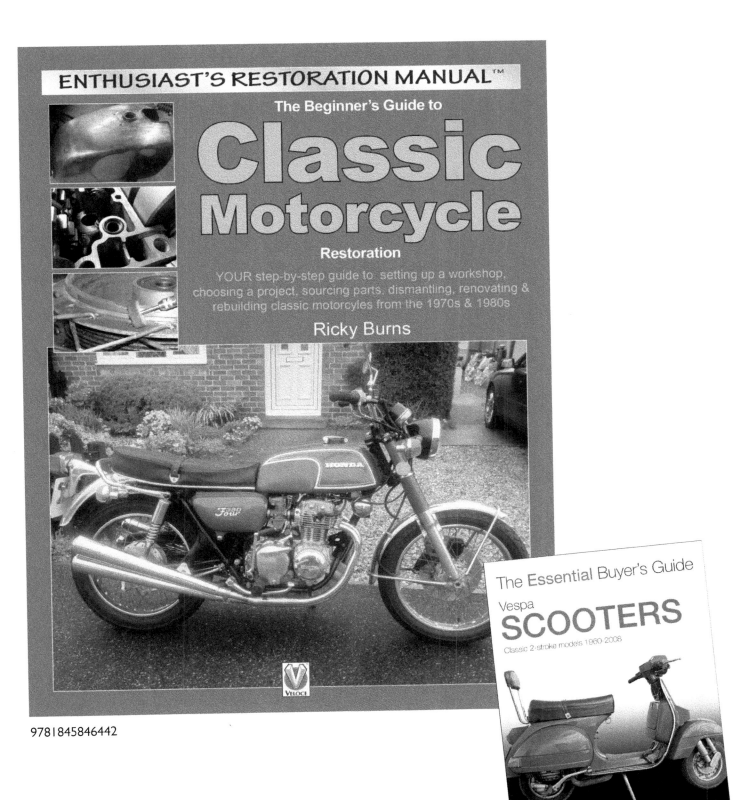

ENTHUSIAST'S RESTORATION MANUAL™

The Beginner's Guide to

Classic Motorcycle

Restoration

YOUR step-by-step guide to setting up a workshop, choosing a project, sourcing parts, dismantling, renovating & rebuilding classic motorcyles from the 1970s & 1980s

Ricky Burns

9781845846442

The Essential Buyer's Guide

Vespa
SCOOTERS

Classic 2-stroke models 1960-2008

9781845848835

Your marque expert: Mark Paxton

Index

For a full listing & details of all our titles please visit – www.veloce.com
All current books • New book news • Special offers • Gift vouchers • Forum